Writing the Critical Essay

GENETIC ENGINEERING

An OPPOSINGVIEWPOINTS® Guide

Lauri S. Friedman, *Book Editor*

Christine Nasso, *Publisher*
Elizabeth Des Chenes, *Managing Editor*

GREENHAVEN PRESS
An imprint of Thomson Gale, a part of The Thomson Corporation

THOMSON
™
GALE

Detroit • New York • San Francisco • New Haven, Conn. • Waterville, Maine • London

For more information, contact
Greenhaven Press
27500 Drake Rd.
Farmington Hills, MI 48331-3535
Or you can visit our Internet site at http://www.gale.com

LIBRARY OF CONGRESS CATALOGING-IN-PUBLICATION DATA

Genetic engineering / Lauri S. Friedman, book editor.
   p. cm. — (Writing the critical essay)
  Includes bibliographical references and index.
  ISBN-13: 978-0-7377-3857-5 (hardcover)
  1. Genetic engineering—Juvenile literature. 2. Genetic engineering—Moral and ethical aspects—Juvenile literature. I. Friedman, Lauri S.
  QH442.G44316 2008
  174'.957—dc22
                       2007032400

ISBN-10: 0-7377-3857-X (hardcover)
Printed in the United States of America

CONTENTS

Examining the state of writing and how it is taught in the United States was the official purpose of the National Commission on Writing in America's Schools and Colleges. The commission, made up of teachers, school administrators, business leaders, and college and university presidents, released its first report in 2003. "Despite the best efforts of many educators," commissioners argued, "writing has not received the full attention it deserves." Among the findings of the commission was that most fourth-grade students spent less than three hours a week writing, that three-quarters of high school seniors never receive a writing assignment in their history or social studies classes, and that more than 50 percent of first-year students in college have problems writing error-free papers. The commission called for a "cultural sea change" that would increase the emphasis on writing for both elementary and secondary schools. These conclusions have made some educators realize that writing must be emphasized in the curriculum. As colleges are demanding an ever-higher level of writing proficiency from incoming students, schools must respond by making students more competent writers. In response to these concerns, the SAT, an influential standardized test used for college admissions, required an essay for the first time in 2005.

Books in the Writing the Critical Essay: An Opposing Viewpoints Guide series use the patented Opposing Viewpoints format to help students learn to organize ideas and arguments and to write essays using common critical writing techniques. Each book in the series focuses on a particular type of essay writing—including expository, persuasive, descriptive, and narrative—that students learn while being taught both the five-paragraph essay as well as longer pieces of writing that have an opinionated focus. These guides include everything necessary to help students research, outline, draft, edit, and ultimately write successful essays across the curriculum, including essays for the SAT.

Using Opposing Viewpoints

This series is inspired by and builds upon Greenhaven Press's acclaimed Opposing Viewpoints series. As in the parent series, each book in the Writing the Critical Essay series focuses on a timely and controversial social issue that provides lots of opportunities for creating thought-provoking essays. The first section of each volume begins with a brief introductory essay that provides context for the opposing viewpoints that follow. These articles are chosen for their accessibility and clearly stated views. The thesis of each article is made explicit in the article's title and is accentuated by its pairing with an opposing or alternative view. These essays are both models of persuasive writing techniques and valuable research material that students can mine to write their own informed essays. Guided reading and discussion questions help lead students to key ideas and writing techniques presented in the selections.

The second section of each book begins with a preface discussing the format of the essays and examining characteristics of the featured essay type. Model five-paragraph and longer essays then demonstrate that essay type. The essays are annotated so that key writing elements and techniques are pointed out to the student. Sequential, step-by-step exercises help students construct and refine thesis statements; organize material into outlines; analyze and try out writing techniques; write transitions, introductions, and conclusions; and incorporate quotations and other researched material. Ultimately, students construct their own compositions using the designated essay type.

The third section of each volume provides additional research material and writing prompts to help the student. Additional facts about the topic of the book serve as a convenient source of supporting material for essays. Other features help students go beyond the book for their research. Like other Greenhaven Press books, each book in the Writing the Critical Essay series includes bibliographic listings of relevant periodical articles, books, Web sites, and organizations to contact.

Writing the Critical Essay: An Opposing Viewpoints Guide will help students master essay techniques that can be used in any discipline.

How Far Should We Take Genetic Engineering Technology?

Ever since advanced genetic techniques were unveiled in the 1990s, society has been talking about genetic engineering. At its most basic level, genetic engineering is the manipulation of genetic material called DNA to change hereditary traits or produce biological products. At present, only some genetic engineering techniques are actually used; genetically modifying plant seeds to produce disease-resistant crops, for example, is one of the most widely used applications of genetic engineering technology.

Though it has only minimally been applied to humans, there is already both great excitement and concerned opposition regarding what implications such procedures might have for humanity. On the one hand, proponents of genetic engineering believe it could lead to a world of reduced disease, birth defects, and greater satisfaction for humanity. After all, the entire struggle of life is focused around improving our place in the world, whether it be taking action to stay fit, move up the job ladder, or getting a higher degree to gain the advantage in a competitive profession. Some believe these improvements should begin at the biological level. As one author puts it, "We can welcome human enhancement, aiming for a future society whose inhabitants can lead flourishing lives of unprecedented scope and capability."[1]

Yet others warn that introducing genetic engineering could herald a dystopia that would have drastic consequences for society, even challenging the very nature of what it means to be human. They fear that selecting human traits gives

[1] Russell Blackford, "Debunking the Brave New World," BetterHumans.com, March 24, 2004.

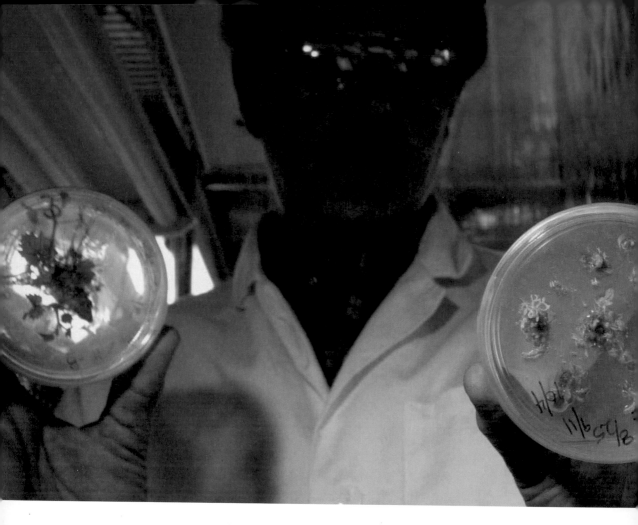

David Gilchrist of the Center for Engineering Plants and Resistance against Pathogens displays genetically modified grape (left) and tomato plants.

humans too much power and could have serious biological and social consequences. Mark S. Frankel, the director of the Program on Scientific Freedom, Responsibility, and Law at the American Association for the Advancement of Science, warns that genetic engineering could "lead us to devalue various social and environmental factors that influence human development in concert with genes. ... A preoccupation with genetic enhancement may place too much emphasis on the genes and ultimately prevent us from solving problems that are really embedded in the structure of our society."[2]

[2] Mark S. Frankel, "Inheritable Genetic Modification and a Brave New World," *Hastings Center Report,* vol. 33, March/April 2003.

At the heart of the debate between these two perspectives is to what extent humans should use science to improve their lives. In many ways, Americans have already accepted science and technology's help towards living longer, healthier, and more comfortable lives. Benefiting from artificial enhancement is increasingly popular, whether it be getting a cavity filled or using contact lenses or undergoing plastic surgery. For example, every year about 700,000 Americans get lasik eye surgery, which corrects vision using laser technology, and that number grows every year. Similarly, thousands of Americans get hip replacements, knee refurbishments, and other joint/organ replacement surgeries that involve high tech procedures and equipment. In the opinion of author Chuck Klosterman, these post-birth adjustments are a stone's throw from making improvements on the genetic level. Writes Klosterman: "The simple truth is that we're already cyborgs, more or less. Our mouths are filled with silver. Our nearsighted corneas are repaired with surgical lasers. Almost 40 percent of Americans now have prosthetic limbs. We seem to have no qualms about making post-birth improvements to our feeble selves. Why are we so uncomfortable with pre-birth improvement?"[3]

But others argue that inputting changes to humans at the genetic level crosses a serious and troubling moral line. Indeed, there are severe social implications to designing humans to have blue eyes or brown hair or be a certain height, weight, or intelligence. It is feared that certain traits will be bred out entirely, a nod to what is known as eugenics. The idea behind eugenics is to improve humanity by breeding out undesirable qualities and selective breeding for positive traits. But who is to decide what constitutes a positive or negative trait? Being tall or short, blue-eyed or brown-eyed, male or female, musically or mathematically gifted—these are all subjective characteristics. And what if humans were all bred towards the same traits? Humanity

---

3 Chuck Klosterman, "The awe-inspiring majesty of science: if tampering with the DNA of unborn children in an attempt to grant them unfathomable superpowers is wrong, I don't wanna be right." *Esquire*, October 2004, p. 108–110.

would quickly lose the diversity that makes us capable of doing different things. If everyone had the same traits, what kind of humans would we be?

Historically, eugenics has been used as a justification for discrimination, human rights violations, and even genocide. During Word War II, for example, the Nazis envisioned a society where everyone was of the Aryan race. To this end, they embarked on a wide-scale killing program to eliminate from the gene pool DNA they considered to be undesirable, such as that of Jews, Gypsies, homosexuals, and others. The Nazis also conducted forced sterilization procedures of persons who appeared to have genetic defects, such as downs syndrome. The Nazis' eugenic vision is an excellent reminder of why it is dangerous to give humans power over selecting traits; it is essentially saying that anyone who does not fit into a preconceived model of what a person should be is expendable.

Despite their significance, it may be too early to ask these large philosophical questions, according to some who believe that the scientific community wastes its time debating whether genetic engineering should be used for human enhancement. For one, despite the enormous amount of debate devoted to the topic, scientists have never attempted to use genetic engineering to improve the human race or to "design" babies with superior traits such as increased intelligence or pleasing physical attributes. There is much doubt that it is even possible in this lifetime. Pre-implantation genetic diagnosis (PGD), the currently-used technique that allows scientists to reduce the risk of hereditary disease in pre-implanted embryos, can only be used to look at a couple genes at a time. But more superficial character traits—such as height, weight, intelligence, skin or eye color—are determined by many combinations of genes, and it will be quite some time before scientists are able to isolate and successfully manipulate them, if ever. As one author reminds us, "There will always be a risk that genetic technology will be

Some people consider genetically modified food to be unsafe. This group gathered outside of Kellogg Company headquarters in Michigan on October 31, 2000, to protest the use of genetically modified crops in Kellogg's products.

hijacked to create designer children. But for now, the technical difficulties make it unlikely anyone will be able to create a true designer baby in the near future."[4]

Whether science will one day catch up to the debate over whether or not genetic engineering technology should be used for the enhancement of humans remains to be seen. However, it is clear that scientists, politicians, religious leaders, philosophers, and others will continue to debate how the technology should be applied, even if only hypothetically. *Writing the Critical Essay: An Opposing Viewpoints Guide: Genetic Engineering* exposes readers to the basic arguments made about genetic engineering and helps them develop tools to craft their own essays on the subject.

[4] "Who's afraid of designer babies?" BBC, http ://www.bbc.co.uk/sn/tvradio/programmes/horizon/babies_prog_summary.shtml.

Section One: Opposing Viewpoints on Genetic Engineering

Genetic Engineering Benefits Humans

Russell Blackford

In the following viewpoint, author Russell Blackford examines the nature of human happiness and concludes that genetic engineering can benefit humans. He considers the story of *Brave New World*, a dystopia about a society in which people have been genetically enhanced and no longer experience human emotions of happiness and love. Blackford says that as long as genetic enhancements help life flourish and assist humans with the things they'd like to be better at, humanity is not in danger of becoming a *Brave New World*. As long as genetic enhancements do not violate or erode the qualities that define what it is to be human, Blackford concludes that genetic engineering will help humanity overcome limitations that keep people primitive.

Russell Blackford is an Australian writer, literary and cultural critic, and student of philosophy and bioethics. His columns frequently appear on BetterHumans.com, a website that advocates scientific enhancement of human beings.

Consider the Following Questions:
1. Why, according to Gregory Stock, will today's humans seem primitive in a thousand years?
2. List 5 qualities that Martha Nussbaum believes are quintessentially human.
3. Why, in Blackford's opinion, does genetic enhancement not threaten the humanity of people?

Russell Blackford, "Debunking the Brave New World," BetterHumans.com, March 24, 2004. Reproduced by permission of the author.

Some of us welcome the prospect of a future in which technology continues to change our minds and bodies, expanding our choices and capabilities. But that is not a universally accepted view. There are many opponents who concentrate on the possible abuses (as they see them) of enhancement technologies and suggest that a future in which we increasingly overcome our biological limitations will be a terrible time to live.

An initial response to them is that our descendants (or we, ourselves, if any of us live that long) may well be happy in a future society of technologically enhanced people. Indeed, humans of the future will probably recall our time as a relatively primitive one that they would never choose to revisit. Gregory Stock has made the point well in his book *Redesigning Humans*. "A thousand years hence," he writes, "those future humans—whoever or whatever they may be—will look back on our era as a challenging, difficult, traumatic moment. They will likely see it as a strange and primitive time when people lived only seventy or eighty years, died of awful diseases, and conceived their children outside a laboratory by a random, unpredictable meeting of sperm and egg."

Plausible though this is, it is not the end of the story. Even if future humans prefer their society and way of life to ours, will they be right to do so?

Understanding Human Happiness

Most of the characters in Aldous Huxley's *Brave New World* [who have been genetically enhanced to comprise distinct classes of people with different jobs and skills] consider themselves happy and would not prefer life in any previous

> ## We Already Use Science to Improve Our Lives
>
> The simple truth is that we're already cyborgs, more or less. Our mouths are filled with silver. Our nearsighted corneas are repaired with surgical lasers. Almost 40 percent of Americans now have prosthetic limbs. We seem to have no qualms about making postbirth improvements to our feeble selves. Why are we so uncomfortable with prebirth improvement?
>
> Chuck Klosterman, "The Awe-Inspiring Majesty of Science: If Tampering with the DNA of Unborn Children in an Attempt to Grant Them Unfathomable Superpowers Is Wrong, I Don't Wanna Be Right." *Esquire*, October 2004, p. 108–110.

The geneticist Dr. Gregory Stock argues that genetic engineering can be used to make human beings happier and healthier.

society. Their lives are subjectively pleasant, and whatever desires they feel are satisfied—almost without a glitch. As with the future humans imagined by Stock, the inhabitants of *Brave New World* would be unimpressed by our society. They would be repelled by its instability, frustrations and endless sources of dissatisfaction.

Yet we find the world of *Brave New World* repugnant, and would do a great deal to prevent it from coming about. It seems clear that we cannot judge whether a society is good or bad merely by whether some or all of its inhabitants prefer to live in it, or even by whether their lives seem pleasant to them.

Some Enhancement Is Negative Because It Lacks Value

In the case of *Brave New World,* much of value is missing from people's lives. The society's creators and rulers have set out to maximize social stability. In doing so, they have banished suffering and frustration, but they have also ruthlessly cut out love, friendship, personal challenges, genuine art, most science and all but the most banal kinds of individual achievement....

When we make judgments about whether a real or imagined human society is good or bad overall, we should first consider whether its people are leading flourishing lives....

But what, exactly, is flourishing?

[Philosopher Martha] Nussbaum develops a fleshed-out conception of a flourishing life for human beings, applicable across all cultures and societies. Central to her theory is the claim that we should ask what people are actually able to *do* in the society in question and, indeed, what they are actually able to *desire*. As she writes, "We consider not only whether they are asking for education, but how they are being educated; not only whether they perceive themselves as reasonably healthy, but how long they live, how many of their children die, how, in short, their health is."...

Qualities that Make People Human

Based on these considerations, Nussbaum offers an extensive list of human capabilities:

- Being able to live to the end of a complete human life, as far as is possible; not dying prematurely.
- Being able to have good health; to be adequately nourished; to have adequate shelter; having opportunities for sexual satisfaction; being able to move about from place to place.
- Being able to avoid unnecessary and non-useful pain, and to have pleasurable experiences.
- Being able to use the five senses; being able to imagine, to think and reason.
- Being able to have attachments to things and persons outside ourselves; to love those who love us, to grieve at their absence; in general, to love, grieve and to feel longing and gratitude.
- Being able to form a conception of the good and to engage in critical reflection about the planning of our individual lives.
- Being able to live with concern for and in relation to animals, plants and the world of nature.
- Being able to laugh, to play, to enjoy recreational activities.
- Being able to live our individual lives and nobody else's.
- Being able to live our individual lives in our very own surroundings and contexts.

In Nussbaum's thinking, many of these capabilities overlap and interact, but they are all basic, and a life lacking in any of them, or deprived of opportunities to exercise them, would be an impoverished one for a human being....

Genetic Enhancement Can Improve Human Qualities

It is one thing to make a list of human capabilities and to use them as an indication of the dimensions of a flourishing

Famous physicist Dr. Stephen Hawking. Hawking believes humans will need to use genetic engineering to keep up with increasingly sophisticated artificial intelligence.

human life. But what would be a flourishing life for someone whose capabilities were greater than those possessed to date by human beings? How should we judge a society of future humans who might actually be, in some ways, more than human?

Some passages in Nussbaum's work give the impression that she might be hostile to human enhancement—though as far as I am aware, she has not addressed the issue directly. She certainly argues in many of her publications that the lives of immortal, invulnerable, godlike beings, or of souls in a transcendent Platonic or heavenly realm, would be missing much that we consider valuable.

Even if that is accepted, however, it does not necessitate that we abandon the quest to enhance our cognitive and physical abilities. No matter how much we succeed in enhancing ourselves, we will remain between the animals and imagined transcendent beings. If our capabilities increase, that will not prevent us from leading flourishing lives, though our flourishing will require the exercise of our new or augmented capabilities. If, for example, our cognitive

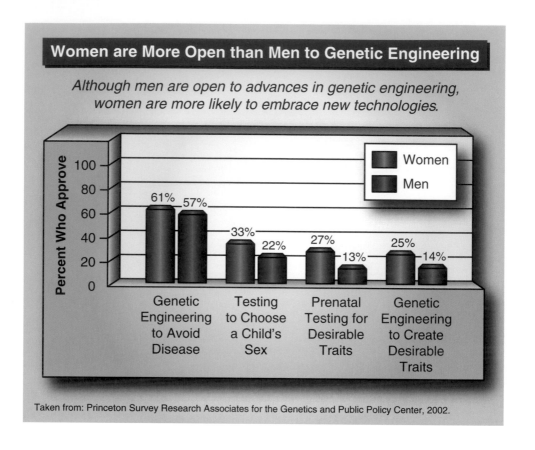

Women are More Open than Men to Genetic Engineering

Although men are open to advances in genetic engineering, women are more likely to embrace new technologies.

Taken from: Princeton Survey Research Associates for the Genetics and Public Policy Center, 2002.

abilities are amplified, we will need projects and activities that challenge them.

Genetic Enhancement Will Help Humanity Flourish

It is in our nature to struggle against our limitations, even if there might be a downside to *total* success. Nussbaum is doubtless correct that we would not prefer a life without, say, hunger to one with both hunger and food. We might not prefer a life of godlike transcendence if we had it, but we have every reason to seek longer and healthier lives than we currently have, including by increasing our bodies' resistance to aging and disease.

Some transhuman futures that we can imagine are, indeed, repugnant to us. A society in which most people were restricted in their choices and activities, and in the horizons of their desires, would clearly be a bad one. Such a society might well emerge if opportunities for cognitive and physical enhancement were monopolized by a self-perpetuating overclass of the rich.

Enhancements Should Assist with Life

However, we need not allow that to happen. We should prevent such a society coming into existence, not by suppressing enhancements of our capabilities, but by ensuring that enhancements become widely available, not restricted to a privileged class. That will involve favoring enhancements that can become common in future societies, which will probably mean, in turn, encouraging those enhancements that could assist people in a wide variety of life plans.

If we adopt that principle, we can welcome human enhancement, aiming for a future society whose inhabitants can lead flourishing lives of unprecedented scope and capability.

Analyze the Essay:

1. In this viewpoint, Russell Blackford defines a principle he thinks should guide the genetic enhancement of humans. What is that principle? Do you agree it is a good guiding principle, or not? Explain your answer.

2. Blackford claims that genetic enhancement will allow humans to perform better while keeping the qualities that make them human intact. How do you think Samuel Hensley, the author of the following viewpoint, would react to this claim? Use evidence from the text in your answer.

Genetic Engineering Threatens Humans

Samuel Hensley

In the following viewpoint, author Samuel D. Hensley argues that parents should not be allowed to choose the characteristics of their children, even if those characteristics would give them some sort of advantage. He discusses the case of Joshua, whose family petitioned to create a brother embryo for Joshua in order to cure a disease he has. Hensley argues that not only is it immoral to create life for the sole purpose of enhancing someone else's life, but the entire process of genetic enhancement threatens the natural social order. For these reasons Hensley opposes processes that allow scientists to pre-screen for diseases and character traits in children.

Samuel D. Hensley is a fellow of The Center for Bioethics and Human Dignity and is a surgical pathologist in the Department of Anatomic Pathology at Mississippi Baptist Medical Center in Jackson, Mississippi.

Consider the Following Questions:

1. According to Hensley, why is the pre-implantation genetic diagnosis procedure immoral?
2. Why does Hensley believe it is unwise to allow parents to select specific traits for their children?
3. What problems does the President's Council of Bioethics foresee with creating designed children, as reported by Hensley?

Samuel Hensley, "Designer Babies: One Step Closer," Center for Bioethics and Human Dignity, July 1, 2004. Reproduced by permission.

A recent *USA Today* article describes the difficulties of Joe Fletcher and his family in Northern Ireland. Joe's son, Joshua, has Diamond–Blackfan anemia, a condition that usually occurs as a spontaneous genetic mutation. If the affected individual reaches reproductive age, the trait is usually heritable as an autosomal dominant disease. Joshua must receive repeated blood transfusions to counteract his inability to produce red blood cells, which carry oxygen to various parts of the body. The only cure for this condition is a stem cell transplant from a compatible donor. Joshua's older brother is not a compatible donor and the chance of any other future siblings being compatible is one in four. The Fletchers hope to improve those odds significantly by using a technique known as *pre-implantation genetic diagnosis*

Daniel Kerner suffers from Batten disease, a fatal genetic disorder for which there is no cure. Scientists believe it may be possible to treat Batten disease using stem cells taken from human fetuses, but this raises ethical questions.

(PGD). The process requires in vitro fertilization. Eggs and sperm from the parents are mixed in a petri dish, and the resulting embryos undergo DNA analysis. Embryos compatible with Joshua could be inserted into the mother's womb to produce compatible siblings. Alternatively, if only a few embryos are compatible, they could be cloned to produce additional embryos in case the first attempt fails to result in implantation and fetal development.

Illegal for Good Reason

This procedure is illegal in Great Britain and is regarded as unethical. Why? Before exploring the British objection, let me add an additional concern from a Christian perspective that regards these embryos as early human life, made in the image of God, possessing unique genes and the capability of continued human development. An important question for Christians is what will happen to the healthy embryos that are incompatible with Joshua. Will they be implanted later and given an equal chance at continued life or will they be discarded? Embryos not selected may be destroyed directly or by destructive embryo research, which is contrary to an understanding of human life being sacred. The *USA Today* article does not mention what plans the parents have for these other offspring.

> # Furthering the Divide Between the Haves and Have-Nots
>
> Promoting a future of genetically engineered inequality legitimizes the vast existing injustices that are socially arranged and enforced.
>
> Marcy Darnovsky, "Embryo Cloning and Beyond," *Tikkun*, vol. 17, July/August 2002.

The British concern expressed previously by the Human Fertilization and Embryology Authority (HFEA) is that human life would be created for the purpose of benefiting others, in this case a brother and the parents. This is a serious ethical concern. Should a child be created specifically to save another person's life, or should a child be welcomed and loved unconditionally regardless of his or her instrumental value in helping someone else? This is important not just from a Christian perspective. Immanuel Kant, the prominent philosopher of rationalism, felt that human beings should always be treated as ends in themselves and not as the means for another person to attain his or her ends. In the Fletcher case, it does not seem that the embryos would be screened to test for known genetic defects. If Diamond-Blackfan anemia is a spontaneous mutation, and no known genetic anomalies are detectable in the parents (such as a mutation for RPS 19 on chromosome 19), then genetic screening is not a helpful option. The decision on life or death then would be made solely on whether a particular embryo, at a later stage of life, might be useful in helping Joshua. This pushes the issue of creating life to serve our needs and wants to a new level, and raises the issue of designer babies.

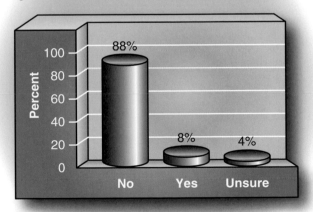

Americans Don't Want Designer Babies

A 2003 Gallup Poll that asked whether parents should be allowed to select traits in their children such as intelligence, height or artistic talent found most Americans oppose it.

Taken from: Gallup Poll, the Gallup Corporation

Parents Must Not Be Able to Choose Their Children's Characteristics

Prenatal genetic testing allows scientists to test established pregnancies for genetic defects that then could be avoided by aborting the pregnancy. Pre-implantation genetic diagnosis allows multiple embryos to be tested and inserted into the mother only if certain *desirable* traits are present. This possibility was recently discussed by Dr. Francis Collins, director of the National Human Genome Research Institute, when he noted that the time may soon arrive when pre-implantation screening will be used to pick desirable traits even in the absence of particular genetic disorders. In the coming years, human genome research will delineate gene clusters associated with increased intelligence, athletic ability, and musicality to name a few. The temptation to redefine parenthood to include choosing particular characteristics in their children, as opposed to unconditionally accepting offspring as a gift of God, seems fraught with perils beyond the scope of this article. For the sake of reflection, let us briefly consider a few issues.

Blastomere biopsy, the process by which a single cell is taken from the embryo for genetic testing, seems safe, but no long-term studies are available to exclude later problems from the procedure itself. In medical research, when new therapies are tested on human subjects, the welfare of the patient is a paramount concern. However, with in vitro fertilization, blastomere biopsy, and genetic screening, the embryos are not considered human subjects even though they are the earliest forms of childhood development and the beginning of lives whose health and well-being will later be a concern to all. Safety for the embryo must be a vital concern.

Designing Children Threatens the Natural Social Order

Our culture has generally considered parents to be the best judges of the welfare of their offspring, but even this has limits. Children are weak and vulnerable; they require

protection from abuse and negligence. The ability for parents to choose which offspring die and which live and what traits they will manifest is an awesome responsibility. The President's Council of Bioethics recently noted that

With genetic screening, procreation begins to take on certain aspects of the *idea*—if not the practice—of manufacture, the making of a product to a specified standard. The parent—in partnership with the IVF doctor or genetic counselor—becomes in some measure the master of the child's fate, in ways that are without precedent ... Today, parents using PGD take responsibility for selecting for birth children who will not be chronically sick or severely disabled; in the future, they might also bear responsibility for picking and choosing which "advantages" their children shall enjoy.

Gillian Woollett (left) and her identical twin Brenda Armstrong. Identical twins share the same genes, making them a natural example of cloning.

Such an enlarged degree of parental control over the genetic endowments of their children cannot fail to alter the parent-child relationship. Selecting against disease merely relieves the parents of the fear of specific ailments afflicting their child; selecting for desired traits inevitably plants specific hopes and expectations as to how their child might excel. More than any child does now, the "better" child may bear the burden of living up to the standards he was "designed" to meet. The oppressive weight of his parents' expectations—resting in this case on what they believe to be undeniable biological facts—may impinge upon the child's freedom to make his own way in the world.

These concerns for tomorrow begin with Joshua's parents today. The proposal is to select purposefully a child solely for his ability to provide a donor source for another child. Creating life primarily to serve someone else, especially when the other life may be rejected and destroyed for the simple reason that it did not meet the parents' needs, is an action that should always be condemned.

Analyze the Essay:

1. Reread the statement made by the President's Council of Bioethics on why genetic selection is dangerous. In what ways do they say it is dangerous for children? In what ways do they say it is dangerous for parents?

2. Russell Blackford, author of the previous viewpoint, and Samuel D. Hensley disagree on whether genetic enhancement helps or hurts humanity. After reading both viewpoints, where do you stand on the issue of genetic enhancement? Do you believe it stands to improve or threaten humanity? Explain your answer in full.

Genetically Modified Foods Are Dangerous

Brian Tokar

In the following viewpoint, author Brian Tokar argues that genetically modified foods are unhealthy, unethical, and threaten natural crop production. Because they are genetically altered to resist diseases, Tokar explains that genetically engineered seeds increase the strength and resistance of disease-causing bacteria, which can have widespread consequences on the health of human and animal populations. Furthermore, he cites studies showing that genetically engineered foods can harm human health. Finally, Tokar takes issue with the notion that genetically modified foods can bring an end to world hunger. Because such foods erode the ability of farmers to plant their own crops, people become indebted to large corporations who can withhold food or charge large fees for it. For all of these reasons, Tokar concludes the use of genetically modified foods is dangerous and threatens humanity's ability to feed itself.

Brian Tokar is a faculty member at the Institute for Social Ecology. He is the author of *Gene Traders: Biotechnology, World Trade and the Globalization of Hunger*. Tokar's articles have also appeared in *Synthesis/Regeneration,* a journal of debate on social and political matters of interest to Greens.

Brian Tokar, "Resisting Biotechnology and Global Injustice," *Synthesis/Regeneration,* fall 2004, p. 13. Copyright © 2004 WD Press. Reproduced by permission.

Consider the Following Questions:

1. According to the author, in what way do companies such as Monsanto seek control over the world's food supply?
2. What did a Scottish scientist find about the health effects of GE foods, as reported by Tokar?
3. What three methods does Tokar say have far more to offer the world's farmers than genetically engineered seeds?

In the summer of 2002, southern African countries facing a threat of growing food shortages shocked the world by refusing a US offer of food aid in the form of GE [genetically engineered] corn. African leaders were concerned about the health consequences for their people, who often rely on corn for upwards of 90 percent of their daily calories, as well as the imminent threat of contamination of local corn varieties if any of the aid corn were to be planted. Several countries ultimately accepted the GE corn, though many required that the corn first be ground into meal to avoid inadvertent planting. Only Zambia, where officials launched a nationwide public debate on GE food, stood firm in refusing this aid.

Worldwide Opposition to Genetically Altered Food

The convergence of biotechnology and corporate globalism once again came into sharp focus in the North in May 2003, when the US announced that it would seek WTO [World Trade Organization] action against Europe's de facto moratorium on approving new GE crop varieties. Literally speaking, Europe as a whole had never legislated such a moratorium. However, no new GE varieties had been approved for import into Europe since 1998, individual

In 2005, Steven Druker helped lead an effort to change Oregon's laws to require that genetically modified food be labeled.

countries were raising increasingly determined obstacles to GMOs [genetically modified organism], and there was a virtual freeze on growing GE crops in Europe, except for a small amount in Spain. Bush administration officials proclaimed that an intervention at the WTO level was necessary to protect American farmers, seeking to paint a populist face on their typically aggressive intervention on behalf of US agribusiness interests....

A History of Crop Failures

Those opposed to genetically modified crops argue that it cuts down on biodiversity, which could have catastrophic consequences in the event of crop failure.

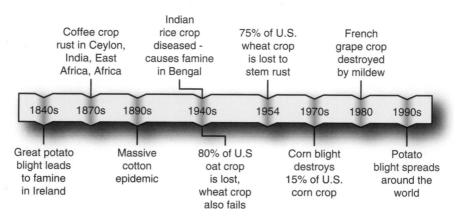

Coffee crop rust in Ceylon, India, East Africa, Africa

Indian rice crop diseased - causes famine in Bengal

75% of U.S. wheat crop is lost to stem rust

French grape crop destroyed by mildew

| 1840s | 1870s | 1890s | 1940s | 1954 | 1970s | 1980 | 1990s |

Great potato blight leads to famine in Ireland

Massive cotton epidemic

80% of U.S oat crop is lost, wheat crop also fails

Corn blight destroys 15% of U.S. corn crop

Potato blight spreads around the world

Why has the technology of genetic engineering inspired such widespread and determined opposition all throughout the world? First and foremost, it is the most visible means by which global corporations are consolidating their control over our food and health, a development that has evolved over several decades. As growing environmental awareness during the 1970s and eighties aroused fears on the part of agribusiness executives that the age of chemical agriculture could be coming to an end, they came to see their possible salvation in the brand new technology of gene splicing, or "recombinant DNA." But the story began even earlier than that.

The Beginning of GE Crops

With pesticide sales increasing a hundredfold since the 1940s, companies like Monsanto, DuPont and Dow had acquired tremendous leverage to advise farmers, and ultimately determine how most of our food is grown. After DDT [a pesticide] was banned in the US in 1972, and prohibitions on other toxic pesticides soon followed, the companies anxiously sought other means to sustain this control. Genetic engineering appeared to be the solution. By shifting their technological interventions right into the genetic makeup of seeds, companies could make farmers highly dependent on new patented seed varieties, as well as on the particular chemicals with which those seeds were "designed" to grow. In the late 1990s, Monsanto alone spent at least $8 billion acquiring several of the leading commercial seed companies in the US and around the world. The company now spends $10 million each year bringing lawsuits against farmers who are believed to be growing Monsanto's GE crop varieties in ways that violate the company's mandatory licensing agreements and patents.

Popular concerns around genetic engineering reach far beyond those directly involved in agriculture, however. Since the introduction of the first commercial GE crop varieties in 1996, independent scientists have discovered a host of disturbing human health and environmental consequences. For example, proteins that cause allergic reactions are passed from one organism to another through genetic engineering, and GE foods may be introducing brand new allergens into our diet, as with the StarLink variety of GE corn that was never approved for human consumption, and forced the recall of well over 300 contaminated US food products in 2000 and 2001.

Genetically Modified Foods Will Not Solve World Hunger

GM-crops have nothing to do with solving hunger; in fact, there is a good chance GM agriculture will lead to a catastrophic famine in the world by greatly decreasing the gene pool of plants and by major disruption of the ecology of life that has evolved over millions of years.

David Kennell, "Genetically Engineered Plant Crops: Potential for Disaster," *Synthesis/ Regeneration*, Fall 2004, p. 11.

A protestor dressed as a genetically altered "Killer Tomato" leads a march to call attention to the safety of genetically modified foods.

GE Foods Are Unhealthy and Unethical

The spread of antibiotic resistance is another unexpected consequence of genetic engineering. Scientists insert genes for antibiotic resistance (so-called "marker genes") as a means to identify the tiny fraction of cells that are "successfully" genetically engineered in their laboratories, and the DNA conferring antibiotic resistance can ultimately be passed along to disease-causing bacteria. A senior scientist working in a Scottish genetic engineering lab discovered even more disturbing effects of GE food on laboratory rats, including a depressed immune response, inflammation of their intestines, and dramatic alterations in the sizes and weights of many vital organs. Overall, very few laboratories around the world have the funds to carry out experiments on GE food effects. Agribusiness corporations have tremendous economic and political leverage over the priorities in agricultural research, and have aggressively intervened to discredit dissenting scientists. Still, every year brings further confirmation of the suspicion that GE foods are harmful to human health.

Genetic engineering also raises a host of other ethical, political, and even cultural and aesthetic concerns. Tampering with the underlying structures of life—by means that overturn the very processes of genetic regulation that help make us who we are—raises alarm for reasons that are sometimes very personal. In the short term, genetic engineering can violate religious strictures against consuming certain foods or combinations of foods, especially where they cannot be clearly identified. But it also raises much wider concerns about the integrity and very meaning of life on earth, whether viewed in a religious or secular context....

GE Foods Do Not Solve World Hunger

The myth that biotechnology is poised to "feed the world" is perhaps the most pervasive of the numerous false hopes that the developers of this technology have aroused. Indeed, people around the world have had to work overtime to dispel this myth, and expose the many ways genetically engineered agriculture is undermining food security and the survival of land-based peoples. In 2001, for example, the world renowned scientist and activist Vandana Shiva denounced the unapproved planting of almost 3000 acres of GE cotton in western India—by a MAHYCO-Monsanto joint venture—as an illegal act of bioterrorism, with no measures in place to protect the region's 130 indigenous cotton varieties from contamination. In 2003, an alliance of indigenous

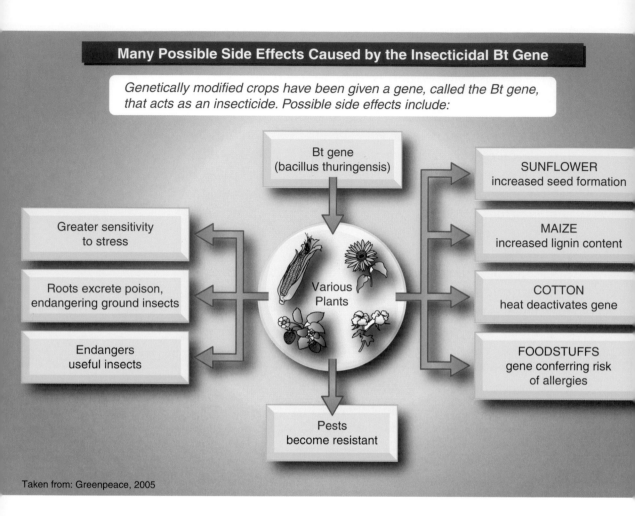

Many Possible Side Effects Caused by the Insecticidal Bt Gene

Genetically modified crops have been given a gene, called the Bt gene, that acts as an insecticide. Possible side effects include:

Bt gene
(bacillus thuringensis)

Various
Plants

SUNFLOWER
increased seed formation

MAIZE
increased lignin content

COTTON
heat deactivates gene

FOODSTUFFS
gene conferring risk
of allergies

Greater sensitivity
to stress

Roots excrete poison,
endangering ground insects

Endangers
useful insects

Pests
become resistant

Taken from: Greenpeace, 2005

and campesino organizations throughout Mexico discovered that the transgenic contamination of ancient traditional corn varieties—which had aroused a worldwide scientific debate when initially discovered two years earlier—had spread to at least 33 communities in nine Mexican states, despite a continuing prohibition against growing GMOs in Mexico. Feeding the world is only possible if people can exercise the fundamental ability and right to feed themselves, and genetic contamination from GMOs threatens this in myriad new and profound ways.... This is especially clear when contrasted with the alternatives. While GE crop varieties have a neutral-at-best effect on crop yields, research combining indigenous knowledge with the scientific application of organic crop improvement methods has led to far more consistent benefits. Crop rotations, natural soil amendments, and detailed studies of the life cycles of various "pest" species—a focus of worldwide research until the dawn of the pesticide era that immediately followed World War II—have far more to offer the world's farmers than the endless cutting and splicing of DNA in pursuit of new commercially viable and patentable "products."

Today's biotech advocates often describe their technology as the harbinger of a "new Green Revolution." With the presumed "benefits" of genetically engineered agriculture far more speculative than those of earlier agricultural technologies, it is essential that their plans continue to be viewed with skepticism and determined opposition.

Analyze the Essay:

1. Brian Tokar describes how activist Vandana Shiva denounced the planting of GE cotton as an act of bioterrorism. What did Shiva mean by this? In your opinion, is the threat GE seeds pose to naturally grown foods serious or exaggerated? Explain your reasoning.

2. Tokar concludes that the only way to eliminate world hunger is to give people the ability to feed themselves. Explain what Tokar means by this, and also why he thinks GE seeds interfere with this ability.

Genetically Modified Foods Are Beneficial

Council for Biotechnology Information

In the following viewpoint published by the Council for Biotechnology Information, the authors argue that genetically engineered (GE) foods are safe, healthy, and can help fight world hunger. Genetically modified crops have been engineered to resist pests and viruses, which will prevent crop loss and ensure plenty of food for farmers and food consumers, the authors argue. Furthermore, GE crops can improve farmers' income by yielding them more crops than non-GE seeds. In this way, GE crops can help fight world hunger by increasing the world's food supply. For all of these reasons, the authors conclude that GE crops are beneficial and should be pursued.

The Council for Biotechnology Information is an organization comprised of biotechnology companies and trade associations that are in favor of plant biotechnology.

Consider the Following Questions:

1. What did a 2002 NCFAP study find about how much additional food was yielded by biotech crops, as reported by the authors?
2. What does *Bt* mean in the context of genetically engineered crops?
3. According to the authors, what will the world's population be in 2030? What bearing does this have on their argument?

Council for Biotechnology, "Good Ideas are Growing: Plant Biotechnology," Council for Biotechnology Information, June 2003. Reproduced by permission.

P lant biotechnology is helping today to provide people with more and better food and holds even greater promise for the future.

Whether cotton farmers in China, India and South Africa, canola farmers in Canada, soybean farmers in Argentina or corn farmers in Spain and the United States, millions of farmers around the world are using biotech seeds to boost yields, improve their livelihoods and preserve the environment. . . .

Papaya farmer Albert Kung checks the leaves on one of his genetically engineered trees in Laie, Hawaii, January 10, 2006.

Types of GE Crops

To date, more than 50 biotech crops have been approved for sale in the United States and Canada, and three have been approved in Mexico. The list includes enhanced soybeans, cotton, corn, canola, cantaloupe, papaya, potato, squash, sugar beets and tomatoes.

Most of these crops have been enhanced in one or more of the following ways:

- **Herbicide tolerant** crops are immune to certain herbicides that are effective against harmful weeds but have no effect on the crop. Globally, about three-fourths of the biotech crops planted in 2002 were herbicide tolerant.
- **Pest resistant** crops usually contain a protein from *Bacillus thuringiensis* or *Bt,* a naturally occurring soil bacterium that wards off the European corn borer.
- **Virus resistant** crops are shielded from plant viruses in a similar way that humans are protected from disease with vaccines: by being "inoculated" and thus building a natural defense. . . .

> ## Genetically Modified Foods Can Alleviate World Hunger
>
> The African continent, more than any other, urgently needs agricultural biotechnology, including transgenic crops, to improve food production. ... East African countries have demonstrated that biotechnology can have a positive impact on hunger, malnutrition and poverty. In some cases, rural farm incomes have tripled as a result of biotech techniques.
>
> Florence Wambugu, Testimony before the U.S. House Committee on Agriculture, Washington D.C., March 26, 2003..

The Benefits of Biotechnology

More and more studies are documenting the economic and environmental benefits of biotech crops.

A 2002 study of biotech crops by the National Center for Food and Agricultural Policy (NCFAP) found that six biotech crops planted in the United States—soybeans, corn, cotton, papaya, squash and canola—produced an additional 4 billion pounds of food and fiber on the same acreage, improved farm income by $1.5 billion and reduced pesticide use by 46 million pounds.

Other global studies have confirmed the economic benefits of biotech crops:

- Yield increases for *Bt* cotton ranged from 5 to 10 percent in China, 10 percent or more in the United

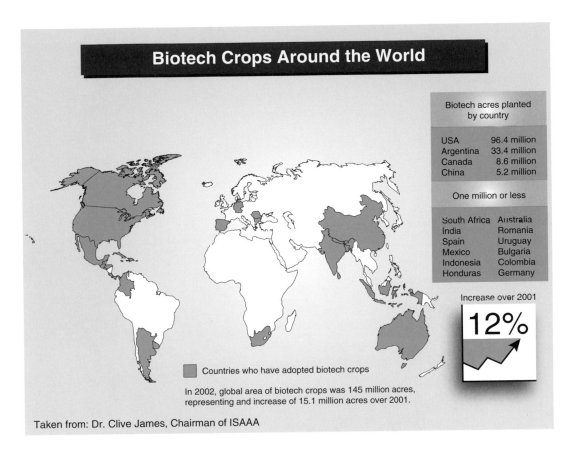

Biotech Crops Around the World

Biotech acres planted by country	
USA	96.4 million
Argentina	33.4 million
Canada	8.6 million
China	5.2 million

One million or less	
South Africa	Australia
India	Romania
Spain	Uruguay
Mexico	Bulgaria
Indonesia	Colombia
Honduras	Germany

Increase over 2001

12%

Countries who have adopted biotech crops

In 2002, global area of biotech crops was 145 million acres, representing and increase of 15.1 million acres over 2001.

Taken from: Dr. Clive James, Chairman of ISAAA

States and Mexico, and 25 percent in South Africa—reaping global cotton farmers an additional $1.7 billion in income between 1998 and 2001, according to ISAAA.

- *Bt* corn in Spain produced yield increases of between 10 and 15 percent—and an average income gain of 12.9 percent—in areas with high levels of insect infestations in 2001-02, according to a study funded by Agricultural Biotechnology in Europe. . . .

Genetically Altered Crops Can Solve World Hunger

With the world population projected to top 8 billion by 2030, there will be another 2 billion mouths to feed—most

Soybeans, corn, cotton and canola are the main genetically modified crops planted around the world.

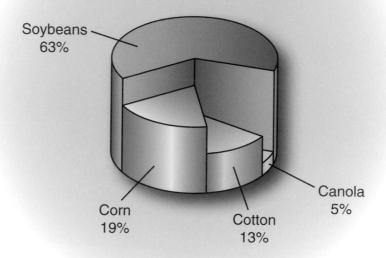

Soybeans
63%

Corn
19%

Cotton
13%

Canola
5%

Taken from: Council for Biotechnology Information, 2003

of them in developing regions. With income growth also fueling demand for better diets, farmers will need to at least double their production over the next 25 years to satisfy these appetites, according to the United Nations. But annual increases in agricultural yields in recent years are holding at just 1.3 percent a year—less than half of the gains of 30 years ago.

C.S. Prakash, founder of the AgBioWorld Foundation, says an additional 4 billion acres will need to come under the plow by 2050 to feed all of these people if there are no increases in farm productivity. That's more than twice the size of the continental United States.

Getting the most production from existing land is important because more than a fourth of the world's 21.5 billion acres of agricultural land, pastures and woodlands have already been degraded from overuse or misuse, such as over-irrigation or erosion. Biologists fear that up to half of the world's remaining 6 billion acres of tropical forests will be lost to agricultural expansion, and some are warning that as many as 20 percent of all tropical forest species could be extinct within 30 years if forests continue to disappear at the current rate.

Biotechnology is not the single solution for feeding a growing population. But it is a tool that can help grow more food in a sustainable way that does not deplete existing farmland or force more remaining wilderness areas to go under the plow.

Researchers are busy developing hardier crops that can produce greater yields on existing land, or even thrive on marginal land:

- A biotech rice that can better withstand droughts and thrive in marginal soil is being developed by Cornell University researchers.
- A biotech sweet potato that can produce twice the yields of conventional varieties is midway through field trials in Kenya. Sweet potatoes are a staple crop for millions in the developing world.
- A biotech papaya—credited with saving the papaya industry in Hawaii—is now being brought to farmers in Southeast Asia, the Caribbean and several other developing areas where papaya is a staple food.

Better food

Not only is biotechnology being used to produce more food, it is also developing better food—food that is healthier, more nutritious and better tasting.

For the developing world, researchers are working to create:

- Golden rice, which is fortified with beta carotene that stimulates the production of vitamin A in the human body. Every year, between 250,000 and 500,000 children go blind because of vitamin A deficiency, according to the World Health Organization. And about half of these children die within a year of losing their sight.

- Cassava, a staple food in many poorer parts of the world, enhanced so it contains 35 to 45 percent more protein and essential amino acids.
- Plant-based vaccines—made from crops such as banana or potato—which are then pulverized and administered in pill form. Researchers have developed a vaccine for hepatitis B that is similar to a traditional vaccine but can be produced by a banana for a fraction of the cost.

It's reasons like these that have led organizations like the United Nations to call biotechnology a "breakthrough technology for developing countries" and the International Society of African Scientists to say that "Africa and the Caribbean cannot afford to be left further behind in acquiring the uses and benefits of this new agricultural revolution."

A Revolution of Super Foods

Biotechnology is also being used to develop better food for people in the industrialized world. Researchers are working to develop:

- A cancer-fighting tomato with three times more beneficial lycopene than conventional varieties. Lycopene protects human tissue and could help prevent breast and prostate cancers as well as heart disease.
- New cooking oils made from canola, corn and soybeans that contain up to 10 times more healthful vitamin E. Researchers believe vitamin E can lower the risk of cardiovascular disease and some cancers.
- Food with fewer allergens. Researchers are working to reduce the allergens in rice, wheat, peanuts and other crops so more of the estimated 50 million people who suffer from allergies worldwide can enjoy the food most people eat everyday. . . .

Dr. Harwig de Haen, assistant director-general of the United Nations Food and Agriculture Organisation, presents a report on genetically modified organisms in 2004. The report concluded that genetically modified crops are safe and have economic benefits for small farmers.

GE Foods Are Safe

Before foods developed with biotechnology can be marketed in the United States, there are nine separate steps in the regulatory process that typically take seven to 10 years to complete—a far more rigorous process than is required for conventional foods, says Bruce Chassy, a professor of food microbiology at the University of Illinois.

"Crops produced through biotechnology have proven to be as safe or safer than crops produced by conventional breeding," he says.

Perhaps the most telling fact about the safety of plant biotechnology is that there isn't a single documented case of an illness caused by foods developed with biotechnology since they first came on the market in the mid-1990s.

Even a report from the European Commission, whose member states are more skeptical about biotech products, concluded that "the use of more precise technology and the greater regulatory scrutiny [over biotech foods] probably make them even safer than conventional plants and foods."

Analyze the Essay:

1. In this essay the authors describe super foods that could be engineered to prevent people from getting sick. Describe some of these foods, and offer your opinion on whether genetically engineered foods are a good way to address vitamin deficiency and other health problems.

2. The authors of this essay contend that GE crops can solve the problem of world hunger. How do you think Brian Tokar, the author of the previous viewpoint, would respond to this claim? List each authors' claims about GE crops and world hunger, and then choose which position you agree with.

Animals Should Be Genetically Engineered

Lester Crawford

In the following viewpoint, author Lester Crawford argues that genetically engineering animals can result in useful products for food, science, and medicine. He discusses technologies that can cause cows to produce different kinds of milk and fish to be more nutritious. In addition, he argues, scientists can use bioengineered pigs and rats to study human diseases and develop treatments for them. While Crawford acknowledges there are risks associated with genetically engineering animals, he insists that the FDA can ensure that the technology is developed safely.

Lester Crawford is the commissioner of the U.S. Food and Drug Administration (FDA) the government agency in charge of making sure America's food and drug supply is safe.

Consider the Following Questions:

1. How does the author say bioengineered pigs have been used to learn about cures for human disease?
2. According to Crawford, what types of genetically engineered mites and mosquitoes are in development?
3. What does the word "Frankenfood" mean in the context of the viewpoint?

Today's biotechnology includes the use of genetically modified animals in medicine; in the production of special foods, human drugs, and medical devices; in the development of animal and industrial products; and in insect-based pest and disease control.

Lester Crawford, "Reaping the Biotech Harvest," *American Enterprise*, March 2004. Copyright © 2004 American Enterprise Institute for Public Policy Research. Reproduced with permission of *The American Enterprise*, a national magazine of Politics, Business, and Culture (TAEmag.com).

Uses for Biologically Engineered Animals

Bioengineered animals are now commonly used for the exploration of medical questions that cannot be readily studied otherwise, such as the mechanisms of both normal physiology and disease in humans and animals. Special pigs, for example, are often used to model human disease, because the size and function of their organs are similar to those of humans. One example is a pig strain bioengineered to test retinitis pigmentosa, a progressive disease that begins with night blindness, and affects between 100,000 and 400,000 people in the U.S. The pig model is intended to help develop drugs to slow the onset and progression of the disease.

Other bioengineered laboratory models include rodents, to study how inborn errors cause disease. Insects and fish are also employed to study disease or population dynamics. *Drosophila melanogaster,* the common fruit fly some of us remember from our college days, is often bioengineered as a model for developmental studies. Transgenic zebrafish and Amazon mollies are used to study effects of ultraviolet irradiation on melanomas.

Making Food More Plentiful and Nutritious

More familiar—and controversial—is the use of bioengineered animals to produce certain foods and medical products. Cows can be genetically engineered to make several kinds of specialized milk. They can produce milk with lower levels of a protein that may make the milk more suitable for up to 6 percent of U.S. infants and others allergic to regular cow milk. They can also produce milk that's more digestible for people who are lactose intolerant; milk that has more naturally occurring antimicrobial enzymes, which increase the milk's shelf life; and milk with altered proteins such as caseins, or with lower water content, which facilitates cheese production. Fish can also be modified to make them more nutritious. One example is the modification of rainbow trout to increase the amount of their omega-3 fatty acids, which can help prevent heart attacks. Within the next few years, we're likely to see many more such products.

Genetic engineering can also develop animals capable of producing therapeutic proteins. In general, these proteins will be produced in the milk of cows, sheep, or goats; in chicken eggs; in the semen of swine; or in blood of various large farm species. The advantage of producing these proteins in animals—rather than in cell or tissue cultures, plants, or microorganisms—is significant. The proteins are better adapted to human use, and the yields are higher. In addition, the post-development costs are lower, because raising a herd of dairy cows is cheaper than building and maintaining a bioreactor facility.

Piglets produced through cloning. Scientists are using genetic engineering on pigs in the hope of finding treatments for human diseases, and possibly developing organs that could be transplanted into humans.

Treating Disease

The production of the protein alpha-1-antitrypsin in sheep's milk is a good example. This is a human blood protein used to treat hereditary emphysema, cystic fibrosis, and chronic obstructive pulmonary disease, believed to affect more than 200,000 people in the U.S. and Europe. This product is already in clinical trials in Europe. Bioengineered animals could also be useful as a source of transplant organs and for medical products such as spider silk made from goat's milk for sturdy sutures, as replacement tendons, or even for bulletproof vests. Genetic engineering of animals is also being used to create faster-growing, bigger, nutrition-enhanced, or disease-resistant salmon, shellfish, pigs, and many other animals. Several approaches are being investigated to modify mosquitoes so they can't spread malaria or certain fevers. There are also techniques that enhance the predatory behavior of certain mites against others that infest plants, which could reduce the use of pesticides.

Anticipating Risks

The Food and Drug Administration is familiar with the risks of biotechnology. We are aware that using genetically altered animals for food raises serious safety concerns that must be addressed through rigorous, science-based analysis. Bioactive compounds are a good example. They include growth hormones, proteins that aid in resisting disease, and even proteins of pharmaceutical interest. If these proteins are present in edible tissues of transgenic animals, they might pose a food safety risk.

Engineering Animals to Serve Vital Societal Interests

Although to date the only genetically engineered animal available on the market is a glowing red aquarium fish, genetic engineering has the potential to address other more vital societal interests. The University of Guelph has developed a genetically engineered pig, coined the Enviropig, that can better utilize feed phosphorus and thus generate 'low-phosphorus manure'; phosphorus from animal manure can contribute to surface water pollution.

Alison L. Van Eenennaam, "Genetic Engineering and Animal Agriculture," University of California, Division of Agriculture and National Resources, Publication No. 8184, Genetic Engineering Fact Sheet 7, 2005. http://anrcatalog/ucdavis.edu/pdf/8184.pdf.

Allergic reactions are another concern. The risk of adverse reactions is raised whenever foods contain new proteins from genetically modified organisms, regardless of whether their source is an animal, plant, or microorganism such as yeast or bacteria.

When it comes to technologies that use viral sequences to introduce new genes, we must consider the possibility that a viral vector used to create some desired trait could recombine with existing viruses in the animal and create a new pathogen. Yet another hazard may arise when the insertion of a gene produces unintended adverse outcomes, known as "pleiotropic effects." These result from the disruption of a cell's normal function, and may lead to cell death. There is also the possibility that biotech products are mishandled through human negligence or error.

The FDA Will Ensure the Safety of GM Animals

How will the FDA cope with the large-scale introduction of products as technologically advanced, highly beneficial, and yet potentially risky as genetically altered animals? We have over a decade of experience in examining more than 50 edible products made from genetically modified plants. The FDA also has a century long record of determining food safety.

Our goal is to make sure that a new product is as safe as its natural counterpart. The FDA has ample experience, as well as legal authority and guidance, for ensuring the safety and effectiveness of drugs, biological medications, and medical devices, and it would use these same resources to evaluate products manufactured with the help of transgenic animals.

But what about other concerns, including the critical question whether, and to what extent, the safety of the environment would be put at risk by genetically altered animals? And what about risks to the animals themselves? The FDA has yet to answer these questions by approving or disapproving the application for marketing of any transgenic animal.

Not much is known about the FDA's vigorous efforts to help ensure the safety of biotechnology. Two years ago [in 2002] we requested that animal cloners withhold any food products made from clones and their progeny until the FDA evaluates potential safety issues. Just like human twins who share the same genome, animal clones are not exact copies, and we need time to collect data for informed decisions about the potential risks these animals may pose to other animals or, as a source of food, to people. We are now finishing food consumption and animal health risk assessments for animal clones, and plan to make them available for public comment. The FDA has also commissioned the National Academy of Sciences to review potential risks of products of genetically modified animals.

The ultimate success of G.M. products is crucially dependent on transparency and producers' communication with the media and the public. The FDA is committed to ensuring that biotech products are safe and that alarming talk about "Frankenfood" is recognized as idle talk that can only do damage.

Analyze the Essay:

1. Lester Crawford is part of the FDA, the organization responsible for ensuring the safety of food and drugs in America. Does knowing the author's background influence the weight you give his argument? If so, in what way?

2. Crawford argues one benefit of genetically altering animals is to allow scientists to discover cures for human diseases. How do you think Jeremy Rifkin, author of the following viewpoint, might respond to this claim?

The cloned calves Bell and Holly, born in February 1998.

Animals Should Not Be Genetically Engineered

Jeremy Rifkin

In the following viewpoint, author Jeremy Rifkin argues against genetically engineering animals. He discusses experiments in which researchers combined different kinds of animals, and focuses specifically on a proposed experiment to fuse a human with a chimpanzee. Although researchers claim to do this in the name of science and medicine, Rifkin believes such experiments breach the natural order, raise difficult ethical questions about what it means to be human, and threaten the survival of the human race. He worries that if human DNA is sprinkled throughout the animal kingdom, there will be a massive breakdown of law and order. In addition to being barbaric and disgusting, Rifkin opposes such experiments on the grounds that they threaten to irrevocably change what it means to be human.

Jeremy Rifkin is the author of seventeen books on the impact of scientific and technological changes on the economy, the workforce, society, and the environment. He is the president of the Foundation on Economic Trends, an organization whose mission is to examine emerging trends in science and technology and their likely impacts on the environment, the economy, culture and society.

What happens when you cross a human and a mouse? Sounds like the beginning of a bad joke but, in fact, it's a serious experiment recently carried out by a research team headed by a distinguished molecular biologist, Irving Weissman, at Stanford University. Scientists injected human brain cells into mouse fetuses, creating a strain of mice that was approximately 1% human. Weissman is considering a follow-up experiment that would produce mice whose brains are made up of 100% human cells.

What if the mice escaped the laboratory and began to proliferate in the outside environment? What might be the ecological consequences of mice with human brain cells let loose in nature?

Weissman says that, of course, he would keep a tight rein on the mice and if they showed even the slightest signs of humanness, he would kill them. Hardly reassuring.

The Bizarre Has Become Reality

In a world where the bizarre has become all too commonplace, few things shock the human psyche. But experiments like the one that produced a partially humanized mouse stretch the limits of human tinkering with nature to the realm of the pathological.

A normal mouse is contrasted with a mouse (left) that was genetically modified to grow large muscles. Researchers hope that studying GM muscle growth in mice will help them develop treatments for human muscle disorders.

This new research field—creating hybrid creatures out of different species—is at the cutting edge of the biotech revolution and is called chimeric experimentation (after the monster of Greek mythology that was part lion, part goat and part serpent).

The first such chimeric experiment occurred many years ago when scientists in Edinburgh, Scotland, fused together a sheep and goat embryo—two completely unrelated animal species that are incapable of mating and producing a hybrid offspring in nature. The resulting creature, called a geep, was born with the head of a goat and the body of a sheep.

For the Sake of Medicine, They Say

Now, scientists have their sights trained on breaking the final taboo in the natural world—crossing humans and animals to create new human-animal hybrids of every kind and description. Already, aside from the humanized mouse, scientists have created pigs with human blood running through their veins and sheep with livers and hearts that are mostly human.

The experiments are designed to advance medical research. Indeed, a growing number of genetic engineers argue that human-animal hybrids will usher in a golden era of medicine. Researchers say the more humanized they can make research animals, the better able they will be to model the progression of human diseases, test new drugs and harvest tissues and organs for transplantation into human bodies.

Some researchers are speculating about human-chimpanzee chimeras—creating a humanzee. A humanzee would be the ideal laboratory research animal because chimpanzees are so closely related to human beings. Chimpanzees share 98% of the human genome, and a fully mature chimp has the equivalent mental abilities and consciousness of a 4-year-old human.

Moral and Ethical Dilemmas

Fusing a human and chimpanzee embryo—a feat researchers say is quite feasible—could produce a creature so human that questions regarding its moral and legal status would throw 4,000 years of ethics into utter chaos.

Would such a creature enjoy human rights and protections under the law? For example, it's possible that such a creature could cross the species barrier and mate with a human. Would society allow inter-species conjugation? Would a humanzee have to pass some kind of "human-ness" test to win its freedom? Would it be forced into doing menial labor or be used to perform dangerous activities? If the whole purpose of creating this hybrid is to perform medical experiments, could those experiments possibly be morally permissible?

Please understand that none of this is science fiction. Anticipating a flurry of new experiments, the National Academy of Sciences, the country's most august scientific body, is expected to issue guidelines for chimeric research in April. What would be the ramifications of creating hundreds, even thousands, of new life- forms that are part human and part other creature? Creatures that could mate, reproduce and repopulate the Earth?

Bioethicists are already clearing the moral path for human—animal chimeric experiments, arguing that once society gets past the revulsion factor, the prospect of new, partially human creatures has much to offer the human race.

> ## The Gruesome Experimentation and Torture of Animals
>
> Among the odd and sometimes grue-some "accomplishments" of researchers: animals that glow in the dark; animals deliberately inflicted with painful deformities; and animals that are hybrids of two or more species. ... These study "participants" are often forced to live out their days in sterile, isolated environments and experience physical deformities, psychological distress, and other problems.
>
> Karen Hirsch, "Brave New Animals," *Animal Issues*, Spring 2003.

Too Much At Stake

Of course, this is exactly the kind of reasoning that has been put forth time and again to justify what is fast becoming a macabre journey into a Brave New World in which all of nature can be ruthlessly manipulated and reengineered to suit the momentary needs and whims and caprices of just one species, the Homo sapiens.

This time, we risk undermining our own species' biological integrity in the name of human progress. With chimeric technology, scientists now have the power to rewrite the

A special biological scaffolding was implanted into this mouse, with human cartilage cells attached. The mouse provided an environment where the cartilage could grow, eventually replacing the scafolding and taking the shape of a human outer ear, which could then be transplanted to someone whose ear was damaged.

evolutionary saga—to sprinkle parts of Homo sapiens into the rest of the animal kingdom as well as fuse parts of other species into our own genome and even to create new human subspecies and super-species. Are we on the cusp of a biological renaissance, as some believe, or sowing the seeds of our own destruction?

What scientists fail to mention is that there are other equally promising and less invasive alternatives to these bizarre experiments. There's sophisticated computer modeling to study disease and to test the effectiveness and toxicity of drugs. There's in vitro tissue culture, nanotechnology and artificial prostheses to substitute for human tissue and organs. When it comes to chimeric experimentation, then, the question is, at what price?

I believe the price is too steep. We should draw the line at this type of experimentation and prohibit any further research into creating human-animal chimeras.

Analyze the Essay:

1. In this essay, Jeremy Rifkin challenges the idea that chimeric experimentation is necessary and suggests alternative ways to study disease and organ transplants. What are some of these suggestions? In your opinion, could Rifkin's alternatives work? Explain your answer.

2. Authors Jeremy Rifkin and Lester Crawford disagree on whether genetically engineering animals can result in positive medical discoveries for humanity. Based on what you know of this subject, what is your opinion on whether animals should be genetically engineered? Is this practice barbaric and unethical or can it positively impact human life? Cite evidence from the text in your answer.

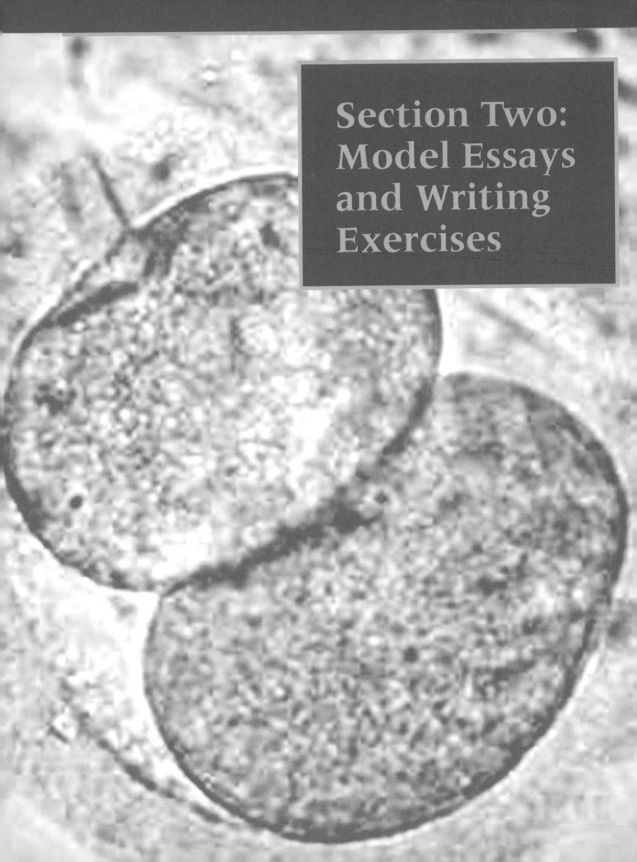

**Section Two:
Model Essays
and Writing
Exercises**

The Five-Paragraph Essay

An *essay* is a short piece of writing that discusses or analyzes one topic. The five-paragraph essay is a form commonly used in school assignments and tests. Every five-paragraph essay begins with an *introduction,* ends with a *conclusion,* and features three *supporting paragraphs* in the middle.

The Thesis Statement. The introduction includes the essay's thesis statement. The thesis statement presents the argument or point the author is trying to make about the topic. The essays in this book all have different thesis statements because they are making different arguments about genetic engineering.

The thesis statement should clearly tell the reader what the essay will be about. A focused thesis statement helps determine what will be in the essay; the subsequent paragraphs are spent developing and supporting its argument.

The Introduction. In addition to presenting the thesis statement, a well-written introductory paragraph captures the attention of the reader and explains why the topic being explored is important. It may provide the reader with background information on the subject matter or feature an anecdote that illustrates a point relevant to the topic. It could also present startling information that clarifies the point of the essay or put forth a contradictory position that the essay will refute. Further techniques for writing an introduction are found later in this section.

The Supporting Paragraphs. The introduction is then followed by three (or more) supporting paragraphs. These are the main body of the essay. Each paragraph presents and develops a *subtopic* that supports the essay's thesis statement. Each subtopic is spearheaded by a topic sentence and supported by its own facts, details, and examples. The writer can use various kinds of supporting material and details to back up the topic of each supporting paragraph. These may include statistics, quotations from people with special knowledge or expertise, historic facts, and anecdotes. A rule of writing is that specific and concrete examples are more convincing than vague, general, or unsupported assertions.

The Conclusion. The conclusion is the paragraph that closes the essay. Its function is to summarize or reiterate the main idea of the essay. It may recall an idea from the introduction or briefly examine the larger implications of the thesis. Because the conclusion is also the last chance a writer has to make an impression on the reader, it is important that it not simply repeat what has been presented elsewhere in the essay but close it in a clear, final, and memorable way.

Although the order of the essay's component paragraphs is important, they do not have to be written in the order presented here. Some writers like to decide on a thesis and write the introduction paragraph first. Other writers like to focus first on the body of the essay, and write the introduction and conclusion later.

Pitfalls to Avoid

When writing essays about controversial issues such as genetic engineering, it is important to remember that disputes over the material are common precisely because there are many different perspectives. Remember to state your arguments in careful and measured terms. Evaluate your topic fairly—avoid overstating negative qualities of one perspective or understating positive qualities of another. Use examples, facts, and details to support any assertions you make.

The Expository Essay

The previous section of this book provided you with samples of writings on genetic engineering. All made arguments or advocated a particular position about genetic engineering and related topics. All included elements of expository writing as well. The purpose of expository writing is to inform the reader about a particular subject matter. Sometimes a writer will use exposition to simply communicate knowledge; at other times, he or she will use exposition to persuade a reader of a particular point of view.

Types of Expository Writing

There are several different types of expository writing. Examples of these types can be found in the viewpoints in the preceding chapter. The list below provides some ideas on how exposition could be organized and presented. Each type of writing could be used separately or in combination in five-paragraph essays.

- *Definition*. A definition essay explains the meaning or significance of the topic you are writing about. Definitions can be encompassed in a sentence or paragraph. At other times, definitions may take a paragraph or more. The act of defining some topics—especially abstract concepts—can sometimes serve as the focus of entire essays. An example of definition is found in Viewpoint 5 by Lester Crawford. He opens his essay by defining the ways in which animals have been biologically engineered, and then moves on to make arguments about this process.

- *Classification*. A classification essay describes and clarifies relationships between things by placing them in different categories, based on their similarities and differences. This can be a good way of organizing and presenting information.
- *Process*. A process essay looks at how something is done. The writer presents events or steps in a chronological or ordered sequence of steps. Process writing can either inform the reader of a past event or process by which something was made, or instruct the reader on how to do something.
- *Illustration*. Illustration is one of the simplest and most common patterns of expository writing. Simply put, it explains by giving specific and concrete examples. It is an effective technique for making one's writing both more interesting and more intelligible. An example of illustration is found in Viewpoint 2 by Samuel Hensley. He uses the case of Joshua to illustrate why genetic engineering is immoral.
- *Problem/Solution*. Problem/Solution is a writing approach in which the author raises a problem or a question, then uses the rest of the paragraph or essay to answer the question or provide possible resolutions to the problem. It can be an effective way of drawing in the reader while imparting information to him/her. The authors of Viewpoint 4, for example, use problem/solution to argue that genetically modified foods are beneficial. They raise the problem of world hunger and propose solving that problem using genetically modified foods and seeds.

Words and Phrases Common to Expository Essays

accordingly

because

consequently

clearly

first…second…third…

for example

for this reason

from this perspective

furthermore

evidently

however

indeed

it is important to understand

it makes sense to

it seems as though

it then follows that

moreover

next

since

subsequently

therefore

this is why

thus

Genetic Engineering Is Unethical

Editor's Notes The first model essay is an "illustration" expository essay that explains why the author believes genetic engineering is unethical. Each paragraph contains supporting details and information, much of which was taken from resources found in Section I and Section III of this book. The essay concludes with a paragraph that restates the essay's main idea—that using genetic engineering in a variety of ways constitutes a breach of morality and ethics.

As you read this essay, pay attention to its components and how it is organized. Also note that all sources are cited using Modern Language Association (MLA) style. For more information on how to cite your sources see Appendix C. In addition, consider the following:

- How does the introduction engage the reader's attention?
- What pieces of supporting evidence are used to back up the essay's arguments?
- What purpose do the essay's quotes serve?
- How does the author transition from one idea to another?

Refers to thesis and topic sentences

Refers to supporting details

Paragraph 1

Enhanced vision. Immunity from disease. Crops that are pest-resistant. These are but a few of the wonders genetic engineering promises to bestow upon humanity. People get swept up in the sci-fi wonder of genetic engineering, but fail to pause and consider the steep price of these technological breakthroughs. In many cases genetic engineering violates human rights and challenges society's most basic understanding of morality and ethics. The following three

The author begins the essay by trying to grab the reader's attention. Did you find it effective?

This is the essay's thesis statement. It tells the reader what the essay will be about.

Editor's Note: In applying MLA style guidelines in this book, the following simplifications have been made: Parenthetical text citations are confined to direct quotations only; electronic source documentation in the Works Cited list omits date of access, page ranges, and some detailed facts of publication.

examples illustrate why genetic engineering is unethical and should be opposed.

Paragraph 2

Why do you think the author included the information about where Hensley works?

Author Samuel D. Hensley, a fellow at the Center for Bioethics and Human Dignity, offers one illustration of why genetic engineering is unethical. He describes a young boy named Joshua Fletcher, whose family petitioned to create a brother embryo for Joshua in order to cure a disease he suffers from. Although the family has Joshua's best interests at heart, they have proposed creating human life for the sole purpose of advantaging others. "Should a child be created specifically to save another person's life," Hensley asks, "or should a child be welcomed and loved unconditionally regardless of his or her instrumental value in helping someone else?" The very basic principles of our society tell us that every being is unique and born with inalienable rights; yet creating a person for the use of another person seems to at once violate these important foundational rules. As Hensley concludes, "Creating life primarily to serve someone else ... should always be condemned."

These quotes are taken from Viewpoint 2. Note how the author of this essay took care to make sure to give credit to Hensley for these statements.

Paragraph 3

This is the topic sentence of paragraph 3. It tells the reader what this paragraph is about: why the genetic engineering of animals is immoral.

Another scenario that illustrates why genetic engineering is unethical is brought to our attention by author Jeremy Rifkin, who discusses experiments in which scientists have used genetic engineering to combine different types of animals, and even to combine animal genes with human genes. Rifkin describes experiments that have attempted to give mice human brain cells, fused together goats and sheep (resulting in a perversion of an animal called a "geep") and tried to create a human-chimpanzee hybrid called a chimera. The immorality of such experiments is obvious: they breach the natural order, raise difficult ethical questions about what it means to be human, and even threaten the survival of the entire human race. Rifkin warns that the chimera and other genetically engineered creatures have the potential to "produce a creature so human that questions regarding its moral and legal status would throw 4,000 years of ethics into utter chaos." (B11).

This quote was taken from Viewpoint 6. What point does it lend support to?

Paragraph 4

A final way in which to illustrate the immorality of genetic engineering is to highlight the gross social inequity it would foster. Indeed, genetic engineering to enhance peoples' physical abilities would likely intensify the already deep divides in American culture. It is no secret that minorities are already at a disadvantage in society; according to the U.S. Census Bureau, both African-Americans and Hispanics on average earn less than white Americans. In 2005, the average white household earned $48,554 while Hispanic households earned $35,967; African-American households earned just $30,858. Such disparities in income already mean that minorities are less likely to become homeowners, less likely to live in neighborhoods with good school districts, and less likely to afford other things that might give them an edge in this increasingly competitive society. Genetic engineering enhancements would likely be afforded by the white and wealthy, giving them another advantage—and a drastic one—over minorities. The disadvantages of this would be enormously unfair, threatening to split society into those who can afford to be genetically enhanced and those who could not. As one researcher worries, "As the genomic future fast approaches, is society in danger of perpetuating unjust inequalities in a way that may destabilize the social order?" (Mwase 84) The divide between the haves and have-nots is already a serious problem in America; offering genetic enhancements only to the small sector of population who could afford them could have disastrous social consequences.

This is the topic sentence of paragraph 4.

These facts support the author's argument that disparity is already a problem in American society.

In what ways has illustration been used in this essay? See Preface B for more information on expository essay types.

Note how the conclusion drives the point of the essay home without repeating material that came earlier.

Paragraph 5

These are just three ways in which genetic engineering threatens to send society down a moral precipice from which it could never recover. For the sake of our children, our animals, our plants, and our citizens, we should eschew the sci-fi lure of genetic engineering and look for more ethical ways to improve society.

Works Cited

Hensley, Samuel. "Designer Babies: One Step Closer." Center for Bioethics and Human Dignity, 1 July 2004.

Mwase, Isaac M. "Genetic Enhancement and the Fate of the Worse Off." *Kennedy Institute of Ethics Journal* Johns Hopkins University Press, Vol. 15, No. 1, 2005: 83–89.

Rifkin, Jeremy. "A Man or a Mouse? Or Both? Efforts to Make Human-Animal Hybrids Must Be Stopped." *Los Angeles Times* 22 Mar. 2005: B11.

Exercise 1A: Create an Outline from an Existing Essay

It often helps to create an outline of the five-paragraph essay before you write it. The outline can help you organize the information, arguments, and evidence you have gathered during your research.

For this exercise, create an outline that could have been used to write *Genetic Engineering Is Unethical*. This "reverse engineering" exercise is meant to help familiarize you with how outlines can help classify and arrange information.

To do this you will need to
1) articulate the essay's thesis
2) pinpoint important pieces of evidence
3) flag quotes that supported the essay's ideas, and
4) identify key points that supported the argument.

Part of the outline has already been started to give you an idea of the assignment.

Outline

I. Paragraph One

A. Write the essay's thesis:

II. Paragraph Two

Topic: Genetic engineering is unethical when it is used to create life for someone else's use.

A. Anecdote of Joshua Fletcher

B. Hensley quote about creating life to serve someone else should be condemned

III. Paragraph Three

Topic:

A. Description of experiments that have attempted to give mice human brain cells, fused together goats and sheep, and others

B.

IV. Paragraph Four

Topic:

A. African-Americans and Hispanics on average earn less than white Americans. In 2005, the average white household earned $48,554 while Hispanic households earned $35,967; African-American households earned just $30,858

B.

V. Paragraph Five

A. Write the essay's conclusion:

Genetic Engineering Can Reduce Disease

Editor's Notes One way of writing an expository essay is to use the problem/solution method. Problem/solution refers to when the author raises a problem or a question, then uses the rest of the paragraph or essay to answer the question or provide possible resolutions to the problem. The following model essay uses problem/solution to show how genetic engineering could help reduce genetically-inherited diseases. The author describes the problem of inherited disease, which plagues hundreds of thousands of American families each year. The author then uses the essay's supporting paragraphs to describe each of the ways in which genetic engineering techniques offer solutions to the problem posed.

Like the first model essay, this expository essay is also persuasive, meaning that the author wants to persuade you to agree with her point of view. As you read, keep track of the notes in the margins. They will help you analyze how the essay is organized and how it is written.

Refers to thesis and topic sentences

Refers to supporting details

Paragraph 1

Each year, thousands of babies are born with debilitating diseases that cause great pain to them and their families. Some are born with poor eyesight and hearing, while others suffer from serious blood diseases such as hemophilia or Tay-Sachs. Autism has become so prevalent that it is estimated that nearly 1 in every 166 children will suffer from it. Still other newborns are laced with genetic bombs such as cancer, which may not go off until much later in life. But new technologies that are capable of identifying genetic diseases can solve the problem of what genetics would otherwise bestow on children. For the good of children, families, and

What problem is established in the introductory paragraph?

What is the essay's thesis statement? How did you recognize it?

society as a whole we should pursue genetic technologies that are capable of reducing disease in our ranks.

Paragraph 2

This is the topic sentence of paragraph 2. It sets the tone for what the paragraph will cover.

Although they sound like the stuff of science fiction, techniques for reducing the prevalence of genetic diseases and disorders in children yet to be born are already available. Indeed, a revolutionary technique known as pre-implantation genetic diagnosis (PGD) can scan parents' genes for devastating genetic diseases, including cystic fibrosis, Tay-Sachs, cancer, sickle-cell disease, hemophilia, neurofibromatosis, muscular dystrophy, and several others. At one fertility clinic in Chicago, PGD has been used to give 200 healthy babies the chance at life without the diseases their parents' genes might have hampered them with. One woman with a family history of early-onset Alzheimer's disease used PGD to ensure her child would not contract the disease by the age of 40, as had happened to most of her family. Without this procedure her daughter might have been condemned to the same fate; or worse, would not have been given a chance at life in the first place, due to her mother's reluctance to bring a child into the world knowing it was doomed to inherit her disease.

What supporting facts, details, and anecdotes are used to bolster the topic sentence?

Paragraph 3

What transitional phrases and words are found in this essay? List them all.

Oddly, many ethical objections have been raised to these practices, but most of these are unfounded. Critics worry that using genetic engineering to manufacture disease-immune children is a breach of the natural order, an inappropriate and dangerous attempt at playing God. They further complain that if efforts to remove diseases from the gene pool are successful, parents may next opt to design children that have more superficial advantages, such as better eyesight or acne-free skin. But it is hard to see why improving on nature could be cause for concern. The entire struggle of life is focused around improving our place in the world, whether

This sentence is part of the author's attempt to persuade you to agree with her. What other persuasive sentences or phrases are found in the essay?

it be taking action to stay fit, moving up the job ladder, or getting a higher degree to gain the advantage in a competitive profession. Why not begin these improvements on the biological level? As one author puts it, "What horrors do such designer babies face? Longer, healthier, smarter, and perhaps even happier lives? It is hard to see any ethical problem with that." (Bailey)

In what way does the Bailey quote support the paragraph's main idea?

Paragraph 4

And when it comes down to it, Americans have already accepted that science can help our lives be longer, healthier, and more comfortable. Benefiting from artificial enhancement is increasingly popular, whether it be a filled cavity or prescription glasses (about 700,000 Americans get lasik eye correctional surgery every year, and that number is growing). "The simple truth is that we're already cyborgs, more or less. Our mouths are filled with silver. Our nearsighted corneas are repaired with surgical lasers. Almost 40 percent of Americans now have prosthetic limbs." (Klosterman, 110) There seem to be few complaints when people make adjustments to themselves after they are born. "Why," asks Klosterman, "are we so uncomfortable with pre-birth improvement?" (Klosterman 110)

What is the topic sentence of paragraph 4? How did you recognize it? How does it support the essay's thesis?

This statement was taken from the quote box in Viewpoint 1. Learn how to spot quotes that can be used to support your points.

Paragraph 5

Using pre-birth genetic engineering techniques in such a way can herald "a future society whose inhabitants can lead flourishing lives of unprecedented scope and capability." (Blackford). Rather than be afraid of such scientific advances, we should embrace this technology for all it can offer us and generations to come. Parents in every era have sought ways to help their children live happier, healthier lives than they did. Why not start from Day 1?

Did the author successfully convince you of her argument? Why or why not? Cite examples from the essay that helped form your opinion.

Works Cited

Bailey, Ronald. "Hooray for Designer Babies!" *Reason* 6 Mar. 2002. www.reason.com/news/printer/34776. html. Accessed September 18, 2007.

Blackford, Russell. "Debunking the Brave New World." BetterHumans.com 24 Mar. 2004.

Klosterman, Chuck. "The Awe-Inspiring Majesty of Science: If Tampering with the DNA of Unborn Children in an Attempt to Grant Them Unfathomable Superpowers Is Wrong, I Don't Wanna Be Right." *Esquire* October 2004: 108–110.

Exercise 2A: Create an Outline from an Existing Essay

As you did for the first model essay in this section, create an outline that could have been used to write "Genetic Engineering Can Reduce Disease." Be sure to identify the essay's thesis statement, its supporting ideas, its descriptive passages, and key pieces of evidence that were used.

Exercise 2B: Create an Outline for Your Own Essay

The second model essay expresses a particular point of view about genetic engineering. For this exercise, your assignment is to find supporting ideas, choose specific and concrete details, create an outline, and ultimately write a five-paragraph essay making a different, or even opposing, point about genetic engineering. Your goal is to use persuasive techniques to convince your reader.

Step I: Write a Thesis Statement.

The following thesis statement would be appropriate for an opposing essay on why genetic engineering techniques such as PGD should not be used to reduce disease:

> Allowing people to design their offspring as easily as choosing wallpaper threatens the very randomness and humility that makes us human: it also threatens to worsen the growing social class divide by offering genetic advantages only to those who are able to pay for them.

Or see the sample paper topics suggested in Appendix D for more ideas.

Step II: Brainstorm pieces of supporting Evidence.

Using information from some of the viewpoints in the previous section and from the information found in Section III of this book, write down three arguments or pieces of evidence that support the thesis statement you selected. Then, for each of these three arguments, write down supportive facts, examples, and details that support it. These could be:

- statistical information
- personal memories and anecdotes
- quotes from experts, peers, or family members
- observations of people's actions and behaviors
- specific and concrete details

Supporting pieces of evidence for the above sample thesis statement are found in this book, and include:

- Statement made by author Samuel Hensley in Viewpoint 2: "The ability for parents to choose which offspring die and which live and what traits they will manifest is an awesome responsibility." This could be used to make the point that parents, or any people, for that matter, cannot be trusted with the responsibility of picking and choosing life.
- Poll results from Section III indicating that 87 percent of Americans oppose allowing parents to use genetic engineering to "design" a baby to satisfy their personal, cultural, or aesthetic desires.
- Quote from box in Viewpoint 2 about how genetic engineering would reinforce the divide between the haves and have-nots: "Promoting a future of genetically engineered inequality legitimizes the vast existing injustices that are socially arranged and enforced."

Step III: Place the information from Step I in outline form.

Step IV: Write the arguments or supporting statements in paragraph form.

By now you have three arguments that support the essay's thesis statement, as well as supporting material. Use the outline to write out your three supporting arguments in paragraph form. Make sure each paragraph has a topic sentence that states the paragraph's thesis clearly and broadly. Then add supporting sentences that express the facts, quotes, details, and examples that support the paragraph's argument. The paragraph may also have a concluding or summary sentence.

How Genetically Engineered Crops Keep Countries Hungry

Refers to thesis and topic sentences

Refers to supporting details

Editor's Notes　Yet another way of writing an expository essay is to use the process method. A process expository essay generally looks at how something is done. The writer presents events or steps in a chronological or ordered sequence of steps. Process writing can either inform the reader of a past event or process by which something was made or accomplished, or instruct the reader on how to do something.

The following model essay uses process to show how genetically engineered crops do not solve hunger problems. The author explains step by step how the use of genetically modified organisms (GMOs) undermines farmers' ability to grow food and keeps hungry countries hungry.

This essay differs from the previous model essays in that it is longer than five paragraphs. Sometimes five paragraphs are simply not enough to adequately develop an idea. Extending the length of an essay can allow the reader to explore a topic in more depth or present multiple pieces of evidence that together provide a complete picture of a topic. Longer essays can also help readers discover the complexity of a subject by examining a topic beyond its superficial exterior. Moreover, the ability to write a sustained research or position paper is a valuable skill you will need as you advance academically.

As you read, consider the questions posed in the margins. Continue to identify thesis statements, supporting details, transitions, and quotations. Examine the introductory and concluding paragraphs to understand how they give shape to the essay. Finally, evaluate the essay's general structure and assess its overall effectiveness.

Paragraph 1

On the surface, genetically modified foods seem to hold the key to better food production. Genetically modified seeds can be engineered to resist disease and to grow under wetter, drier, hotter, or cooler conditions than organic seeds are able. This allows them to deliver a crop even if weather that year was abnormal. Genetically engineered foods, such as fruits and vegetables, can also be designed to have desired properties such as size or color; larger, redder tomatoes, for example, or sweeter corn. But in reality, genetically engineered foods threaten the environment and perpetuate the problem of world hunger. Examining the process by which the use of genetically modified crops keeps hungry countries hungry will help shed light on this critical problem.

Note how the introduction sets a position up in order to then spend the rest of the essay knocking it down. See Exercise 3A at the end of this essay for more ways to craft an essay introduction.

What is the essay's thesis statement? (Hint: it's not the last sentence in paragraph 1).

Paragraph 2

After genetically modified seeds are developed they are patented, or protected under law, as a "product" that belongs to a company that can then license or distribute them. One such company that patents GE seeds is Monsanto, a multinational agricultural biotechnology corporation that holds more than 70 percent of market share for various genetically engineered crops. The patenting of seeds is the first step in the chain of events that undermine world-wide efforts to reduce hunger. Many groups, such as the environmental organization Greenpeace, oppose the idea of a patented life form at all, stating that "Life is not an industrial commodity." (Greenpeace) The Sierra Club also weighs in on this topic, arguing that "the genetic code, which has evolved over billions of years, should remain the shared, common heritage of us all." (Sierra Club)

What sources are quoted in the essay? What are their qualifications? See Exercise 3B at the end of this essay for more information on selecting quotes.

After seeds are patented they are sold to farmers, a second step in the process of environmental, agricultural, and economic ruin. Some of the traits the seeds are infused with can actually ruin a farmer's prospects for future growing. For example, many GE seeds contain a toxin known as Bt, which allows them to be pest-resistant. But Bt can be released into the soil, where it remains poisonous for long periods of time. In this way, even if a GE seed crop is used once, it can ruin the soil should a farmer decide to use non-GE seeds for the next crop.

> What is the topic sentence of paragraph 3? How did you identify it? What pieces of evidence support it?

GE seeds can also ruin a farmer's crop by spreading to nearby crops and ecosystems, threatening ecological diversity. When genetically modified seeds come into contact with organic plants and animals, they threaten the biodiversity of an entire area by dominating other life forms. And seeds can travel: according to the Council for Responsible Genetics, researchers in Australia have discovered that a canola plant can cross-pollinate with a plant from a related species located as far as three kilometers away. Similarly, pollen, insects, and birds help seeds travel for miles. If seeds from genetically modified corn were to spread to a nearby soybean field, for example, the corn seeds could ruin that soil by soaking it with Bt, and kill the soybean crop. Alternatively, Bt might commingle with weeds, helping them become immune to certain pesticides. These weeds might then threaten other plants that keep the local ecosystem in check. For these reasons the Sierra Club worries that genetically modified seeds "might have the ability to outcompete native species in the environment and destroy natural biological systems." Greenpeace dubs this "genetic pollution", warning that "these genetically modified organisms (GMO) can spread through nature and interbreed with natural organisms, thereby contaminating non 'GE' environments and future generations in an unforeseeable and uncontrollable way."

> What facts and statistics are used in the essay? Make a list of all facts and statistics and what points they are used in support of.

Paragraph 5

Why is crop diversity so important? For the same reason that all diversity of life is important: for survival. Relying on just one strain of crop is exceedingly risky, as history has shown. For example, Ireland used to rely exclusively on potatoes to feed its people; but in 1845, when blight killed off the Irish potato crop, over one million people starved to death, and another two million were forced to leave the country. Similarly, if a single strand of genetically modified corn replaces the multitude of strains of corn found naturally, the people who depend on this food could be in big trouble if the crop fails. It is for this reason that "biological diversity must be protected and respected as the global heritage of humankind, and one of our world's fundamental keys to survival." (Greenpeace) When we limit biodiversity, we cut down on the life-sustaining options available to us.

> What transitional words and phrases does the author use to keep the ideas in the essay smoothly flowing?

Paragraph 6

Another way in which GE seeds can ruin farmers' crops is by indebting farmers to a certain corporation. Approximately 70 percent of the world's farmers rely on farm-saved seeds, or seeds that are leftover from a crop, to plant next year's crop. But because GE seeds are patented, farmers are not allowed to use the seeds unless they pay a company like Monsanto for them. In this way, farmers become indebted to huge corporations for the "right" to grow food.

> What is the topic sentence of Paragraph 6?

Paragraph 7

Finally, although it is not yet in practice, Monsanto and its partner companies have patented technology to build into seeds a "self-destruct" mechanism that would kill the seeds after one crop so they could not be used again. This self-destruct mechanism, or "terminator technology," as it is known, would prevent farmers from being able to use seeds to plant a future crop. And, because their soil would likely be soaked with Bt and thus only be able to tolerate a new batch of GE seeds, farmers would be forced back to

> What words and phrases let you know that this is a process essay? Which ones let you know this is a persuasive essay?

the companies, who could sell their seeds for an enormous price. Thus far laws have prevented Monsanto from inserting the self-destruct mechanism into its seeds, but if they were to become able, farmers might find themselves enslaved to GE foods.

Paragraph 8

In addition to each of these destructive steps, it is an absolute myth that genetically engineered foods could provide enough food to overcome world hunger. Indeed, lack of food is not the primary cause of hunger. What contributes more to hunger is an unequal distribution of land and resources. For example, Argentina is the second largest producer of genetically engineered crops in the whole world. But this food is not used to feed Argentineans; Greenpeace reports that millions of tons of soy and other products are exported from Argentina every year to feed cattle in other countries, while millions of Argentineans go hungry.

Paragraph 9

What transitional phrases are used in Paragraphs 8 and 9?

In fact, some of the hungriest countries in the world are food exporters. India, for example, is the third largest producer of food in the world, producing from 40 to 80 million tons of excess food grains in a year: yet there are over 350 million Indians who are starving. Consider too that almost 78 percent of countries with serious child malnutrition problems are food-exporting countries—meaning that the food they produce is traded to other countries instead of feeding their own people. Solving hunger involves allowing them to control their resources, not indebting them to enormous corporations and forcing them to export their food for a profit. Writes one author, "Feeding the world is only possible if people can exercise the fundamental ability and right to feed themselves, and genetic contamination from GMOs threatens this in myriad new and profound ways." (Tokar, 17)

Paragraph 10

Even the world's hungriest people know that genetically modified food will not solve their problems. In 2002 Zambia, one of several southern African nations that face dramatic food shortages, turned down a U.S. offer to provide shipments of genetically-engineered corn. Zambians rely on corn for almost 90 percent of their diet, yet they still turned it down. In addition to fearing the health consequences of what genetically tampered foods could do to their bodies, the Zambians worried that their local corn crops could be contaminated by the genetically-modified seeds. This reality is what caused one author to write: "GM-crops have nothing to do with solving hunger; in fact, there is a good chance GM agriculture will lead to a catastrophic famine in the world by greatly decreasing the gene pool of plants and by major disruption of the ecology of life that has evolved over millions of years." (Kennell, 11)

What is the topic sentence of Paragraph 10?

How does the example from Zambia help underscore the author's point? Why is it especially compelling?

Paragraph 11

Outlining the process by which genetically modified organisms threaten to keep the world hungry is an important part of understanding the threat posed by GE foods and seeds. As one author writes, "Seeds are the first link of the food chain. Control of the seed is control of the food system." (Mittal) The key to preventing hunger is to put control of food in the hands of the farmers, not the corporations. Although using genetically-engineered seeds may appear to reduce hunger, in reality this technology promises to perpetuate the problem of hunger and exploitation all over the world. Bigger, redder tomatoes cannot hide the fact that genetically engineered foods keep the world hungry, and on these grounds should be resisted.

How does the conclusion return to the ideas of the introduction?

Works Cited

Greenpeace. "Say No to Genetic Engineering." < http://www.greenpeace.org/international/campaigns/genetic-engineering> Accessed May 17, 2007.

Kennell, David. "Genetically Engineered Plant Crops: Potential for Disaster." *Synthesis/Regeneration* Fall 2004: 11.

Mittal, Anuradha. "Biotechnology and the Third World: A Question of Social Morality." 5 June 2003. < www.foodfirst.org >.

The Sierra Club. "Banned Abroad, Sold in the U.S.!!! Genetically Engineered Food." 1 July 2001 < www.sierraclub.org >

Tokar, Brian. "Resisting Biotechnology and Global Injustice." *Synthesis/Regeneration* Fall 2004: 13–17.

Exercise 3A: Examining Introductions and Conclusions

Every essay features introductory and concluding paragraphs that are used to frame the main ideas being presented. Along with presenting the essay's thesis statement, well-written introductions should grab the attention of the reader and make clear why the topic being explored is important. The conclusion reiterates the essay's thesis and is also the last chance for the writer to make an impression on the reader. Strong introductions and conclusions can greatly enhance an essay's effect on an audience.

The Introduction

There are several techniques that can be used to craft an introductory paragraph. An essay can start with:

- an anecdote: a brief story that illustrates a point relevant to the topic;
- startling information: facts or statistics that elucidate the point of the essay;
- setting up and knocking down a position: a position or claim believed by proponents of one side of a controversy, followed by statements that challenge that claim;
- historical perspective: an example of the way things used to be that leads into a discussion of how or why things work differently now;
- summary information: general introductory information about the topic that feeds into the essay's thesis statement.

Problem One
Reread the introductory paragraphs of the model essays and of the viewpoints in Section I. Identify which of the techniques described above are used in the example essays. How do they grab the attention of the reader? Are their thesis statements clearly presented?

Problem Two

Write an introduction for the essay you have outlined and partially written in Exercise 2B using one of the techniques described above.

The Conclusion

The conclusion brings the essay to a close by summarizing or returning to its main ideas. Good conclusions, however, go beyond simply repeating these ideas. Strong conclusions explore a topic's broader implications and reiterate why it is important to consider. They may frame the essay by returning to an anecdote featured in the opening paragraph. Or they may close with a quotation or refer back to an event in the essay. In opinionated essays, the conclusion can reiterate which side the essay is taking or ask the reader to reconsider a previously held position on the subject.

Problem Three

Reread the concluding paragraphs of the model essays and of the viewpoints in Section I. Which were most effective in driving their arguments home to the reader? What sorts of techniques did they use to do this? Did they appeal emotionally to the reader, or bookend an idea or event referenced elsewhere in the essay?

Problem Four

Write a conclusion for the essay you have outlined and partially written in Exercise 2B using one of the techniques described above.

Exercise 3B: Using Quotations to Enliven Your Essay

No essay is complete without quotations. Get in the habit of using quotes to support at least some of the ideas in your essays. Quotes do not need to appear in every paragraph, but they should appear often enough so that the essay contains voices aside from your own. When you write, use quotations to accomplish the following:

- Provide expert advice that you are not necessarily in the position to know about
- Cite lively or passionate passages
- Include a particularly well-written point that gets to the heart of the matter
- Supply statistics or facts that have been derived from someone's research
- Deliver anecdotes that illustrate the point you are trying to make
- Express first-person testimony

Problem One: Reread the essays presented in all sections of this book and find at least one example of each of the above quotation types.

There are a couple of important things to remember when using quotations.

- Note your sources' qualifications and biases. This way your reader can identify the person you have quoted and can put their words in a context.
- Put any quoted material within proper quotation marks. Failing to attribute quotes constitutes plagiarism, which is when an author takes someone else's words or ideas and presents them as their own. Plagiarism is a form of intellectual theft and must be avoided at all costs.

Write Your Own Expository Five-Paragraph Essay

Using the information from this book, write your own five-paragraph expository essay that deals with genetic engineering. You can use the resources in this book for information about issues relating to this topic and how to structure this type of essay.

The following steps are suggestions on how to get started.

Step One: Choose your topic.
The first step is to decide what topic to write your expository essay on. Is there any subject that particularly fascinates you? Is there an issue you strongly support, or feel strongly against? Is there a topic you feel personally connected to or one that you would like to learn more about? Ask yourself such questions before selecting your essay topic. Refer to Appendix D: Sample Essay Topics if you need help selecting a topic.

Step Two: Write down questions and answers about the topic.
Before you begin writing, you will need to think carefully about what ideas your essay will contain. This is a process known as brainstorming. Brainstorming involves asking yourself questions and coming up with ideas to discuss in your essay. Possible questions that will help you with the brainstorming process include:

- Why is this topic important?
- Why should people be interested in this topic?
- How can I make this essay interesting to the reader?
- What question am I going to address in this paragraph or essay?
- What facts, ideas, or quotes can I use to support the answer to my question?

Questions especially for expository essays include:

- Do I want to write an informative essay or an opinion-ated essay?
- Will I need to explain a process or course of action?
- Will my essay contain many definitions or explana-tions?
- Is there a particular problem that needs to be solved?

Step Three: Gather facts, ideas, and anecdotes related to your topic.

This book contains several places to find information, includ-ing the viewpoints and the appendices. In addition, you may want to research the books, articles, and Web sites listed in Section III, or do additional research in your local library. You can also conduct interviews if you know someone who has a compelling story that would fit well in your essay.

Step Four: Develop a workable thesis statement.

Use what you have written down in steps two and three to help you articulate the main point or argument you want to make in your essay. It should be expressed in a clear sen-tence and make an arguable or supportable point.

Example:
Parents, doctors, philosophers, and others need not get too hysterical imagining a society in which a child's char-acteristics are ordered up as easy as a fast food order.

(This could be the thesis statement of an expository essay that explains why the debate over whether genetically prescreening babies for desirable traits is moot, because so much of the debate centers on technologies that are not likely to become viable for a long time.)

Step Five: Write an outline or diagram.
a. Write the thesis statement at the top of the outline.
b. Write roman numerals I, II, and III on the left side of the page.

c. Next to each roman numeral, write down the best ideas you came up with in step three. These should all directly relate to and support the thesis statement.

d. Next to each letter write down information that supports that particular idea.

Step Six: Write the three supporting paragraphs.

Use your outline to write the three supporting paragraphs. Write down the main idea of each paragraph in sentence form. Do the same thing for the supporting points of information. Each sentence should support the paragraph of the topic. Be sure you have relevant and interesting details, facts, and quotes. Use transitions when you move from idea to idea to keep the text fluid and smooth. Sometimes, although not always, paragraphs can include a concluding or summary sentence that restates the paragraph's argument.

Step Seven: Write the introduction and conclusion.

See Exercise 3A for information on writing introductions and conclusions.

Step Eight: Read and rewrite.

As you read, check your essay for the following:

- ✔ Does the essay maintain a consistent tone?
- ✔ Do all paragraphs reinforce your general thesis?
- ✔ Do all paragraphs flow from one to the other? Do you need to add transition words or phrases?
- ✔ Have you quoted from reliable, authoritative, and interesting sources?
- ✔ Is there a sense of progression throughout the essay?
- ✔ Does the essay get bogged down in too much detail or irrelevant material?
- ✔ Does your introduction grab the reader's attention?
- ✔ Does your conclusion reflect back on any previously discussed material, or give the essay a sense of closure?
- ✔ Are there any spelling or grammatical errors?

**Section Three:
Supporting
Research
Material**

Facts About Genetic Engineering

Editor's Note: These facts can be used in reports or papers to reinforce or add credibility when making important points or claims.

Genetic Engineering and Humans

Genetic engineering is the manipulation of genetic material (DNA) to change hereditary traits or produce biological products.

- Genetically engineered products include bacteria designed to "eat" or break down oil and industrial waste products; drugs such as hormones and insulin; plants that are resistant to diseases, insects and herbicides and that yield fruits and vegetables with desired properties such as size or color; animals that have been genetically altered to have a specific trait, such as increased milk production.
- Genetic engineering has helped scientists make great breakthroughs in medicine, including cancer research, gene therapy, insulin production, vaccines, genetic testing for inherited disease, and embryonic stem cell research.
- Despite the enormous amount of debate devoted to the topic, scientists have never attempted to use genetic engineering to improve the human race or to "design" babies with superior traits such as increased intelligence or pleasing physical attributes.
- Reproductive Genetics Institute in Chicago offers pre-implantation genetic diagnosis (PGD) for $10,000 ($2,500 for the PGD and $7,500 for in-vitro fertilization of the screened embryo).

Genetic Engineering and Crops

- Approximately two-thirds of processed foods are made with a genetically engineered organism.
- Currently, there are no U.S. laws that state foods that contain genetically modified organisms must be labeled as such.
- The European Union requires foods that contain genetically modified ingredients to be labeled as such.
- Genetically modified seeds can be engineered to resist disease and to grow under wetter, drier, hotter, or cooler conditions than organic seeds are able.
- A plant can cross-pollinate with another plant from a related species located as far as three kilometers away, according to the Council for Responsible Genetics. This could mean that genetically modified seeds could pollute crops that are miles away.
- A 2002 Council for Agricultural Science and Technology found that genetically modified crops result in
  - the adoption of conservation farming techniques
  - the preservation of 37 million tons of topsoil
  - an 85 percent reduction in greenhouse gas emissions from farm equipment and machinery
  - a 70 percent reduction in herbicide runoff
  - a 90 percent decrease in soil erosion
- According to the International Service of Agri-Biotech Applications, more than 27 percent of the world's genetically engineered crops are located in developing countries.
- Opponents of genetically modified seeds often argue that a shortage food is not necessarily responsible for hunger. India, for example, is the third largest producer of food in the world, producing from 40 to 80 million tons of excess food grains in a year: yet there are over 350 million Indians who are starving.
- Almost 78 percent of countries with serious child malnutrition problems are food exporting countries—meaning, the food they produce is traded to other countries instead of feeding their own people.

- Those opposed to genetically modified crops argue that it cuts down on biodiversity, which could have catastrophic consequences in the event of crop failure. Historic crop failures include:
  - The 1840s great potato blight, which led to famine in Ireland
  - The 1870s coffee crop rust in Ceylon, India, East Africa, and Africa
  - The massive cotton epidemic of the 1890s
  - The loss of 80 percent of the U.S. oat crop in the 1940s
  - The loss of 75 percent of the U.S. wheat crop in 1954 to stem rust
  - The loss of 15 percent of the U.S. corn crop in the 1970s to corn blight
  - The obliteration of the French grape crop in 1980 by mildew
- Soybeans, corn, cotton, and canola are the main genetically modified crops planted around the world:
  - 63 percent of biotech plantings are soybean crops;
  - 19 percent of biotech plantings are corn crops;
  - 13 percent of biotech plantings are cotton crops;
  - 5 percent of biotech plantings are canola crops.
- The U.S. leads the world in the planting of biotech crops, with more than 96 million acres of genetically modified crop seeds planted.
- Argentina has 13.4 million acres of biotech crops.
- Canada has 8.6 million acres of biotech crops.
- China has 5.2 million acres of biotech crops.
- The following nations have one million or fewer acres of biotech crops: Australia, Bulgaria, Colombia, Germany, Honduras, India, Indonesia, Mexico, Romania, South Africa, and Uruguay.

Opinions about Genetic Engineering

The American public remains wary of using genetic engineering to "design" their babies. A University of Illinois at Chicago study found that:

- 77 percent of people who wanted more than one child indicated they had no preference as to the sex of their children, or said they would be happy to have an equal number of boys and girls.
- Only 12 percent would use sex selection technology, and it would have to be available in any doctor's office, require only a single cycle of intrauterine insemination, and be covered by health insurance.
- 82 percent of respondents said they would not choose the sex of their child even if it were as simple as taking a blue pill for a boy and a pink pill for a girl. Just 18 percent of respondents indicated they would do so if this were possible.

A 2002 poll conducted by the Discovery Channel in 2002 found that 87 percent of Americans oppose allowing parents to use genetic engineering to "design" a baby to satisfy their personal, cultural, or aesthetic desires.

A 2003 Gallup poll found that 88 percent of Americans disapproved of allowing parents to select traits in their children such as intelligence, height, or artistic talent. Just 8 percent approved, while 4 percent were unsure.

Men and women have similar opinions about using genetic technology, according to a 2002 study by the Genetics and Public Policy Center, which found that:

- 74 percent of men and 73 percent of women approve of testing to avoid serious genetic disease
- 74 percent of men and 70 percent of women approve of in vitro fertilization
- 69 percent of men and 69 percent of women approve of testing to ensure child's tissue and blood matches parents

- 67 percent of men and 66 percent of women approve of testing for disease
- 56 percent of men and 64 percent of women approve of testing to avoid tendency to diseases like cancer
- 22 percent of men and 33 percent of women approve of testing to choose a child's sex
- 13 percent of men and 27 percent of women approve of prenatal testing for desirable traits
- 18 percent of men and 26 percent of women approve of testing embryos to ensure child has desirable characteristics
- 57 percent of men and 61 percent of women approve of genetic engineering to avoid disease
- 14 percent of men and 25 percent of women approve of genetic engineering to create desirable traits

Finding and Using Sources of Information

No matter what type of essay you are writing, it is necessary to find information to support your point of view. You can use sources such as books, magazine articles, newspaper articles, and online articles.

Using Books and Articles

You can find books and articles in a library by using the library's computer or cataloging system. If you are not sure how to use these resources, ask a librarian to help you. You can also use a computer to find many magazine articles and other articles written specifically for the Internet.

You are likely to find a lot more information than you can possibly use in your essay, so your first task is to narrow it down to what is likely to be most usable. Look at book and article titles. Look at book chapter titles, and examine the book's index to see if it contains information on the specific topic you want to write about. (For example, if you want to write about designer babies and you find a book about genetic engineering, check the chapter titles and index to be sure it contains information about designer babies or genetic prescreening before you bother to check out the book.)

For a five-paragraph essay, you do not need a great deal of supporting information, so quickly try to narrow down your materials to a few good books and magazine or Internet articles. You do not need dozens. You might even find that one or two good books or articles contain all the information you need.

You probably do not have time to read an entire book, so find the chapters or sections that relate to your topic, and skim these. When you find useful information, copy it onto a note card or into a notebook. You should look for supporting facts, statistics, quotations, and examples.

Using the Internet

When you select your supporting information, it is important that you evaluate its source. This is especially important with information you find on the Internet. Because nearly anyone can put information on the Internet, there is as much bad information as good information. Before using Internet information—or any information—try to determine if the source seems to be reliable. Is the author or Internet site sponsored by a legitimate organization? Is it from a government source? Does the author have any special knowledge or training relating to the topic you are looking up? Does the article give any indication of where its information comes from?

Using Your Supporting Information

When you use supporting information from a book, article, interview or other source, there are three important things to remember:

1. *Make it clear whether you are using a direct quotation or a paraphrase.* If you copy information directly from your source, you are quoting it. You must put quotation marks around the information, and tell where the information comes from. If you put the information in your own words, you are paraphrasing it.

   Here is an example of a using a quotation:

   Genetic engineering offers us the chance to alleviate the poverty and hunger that runs rampant in developing countries. Scientist and founder of Africa Harvest Biotech Foundation International Florence Wambugu testified before Congress to this effect: "The African continent, more than any other, urgently needs agricultural biotechnology, including transgenic crops, to improve food production." (Wambugu)

Here is an example of a brief paraphrase of the same passage:

> Genetic engineering offers us the chance to alleviate the poverty and hunger that runs rampant in developing countries. Scientist and founder of Africa Harvest Biotech Foundation International Florence Wambugu explains that Africa is one such place where genetically modified seeds could help boost food production and feed thousands of starving people.

2. *Use the information fairly.* Be careful to use supporting information in the way the author intended it. For example, it is unfair to quote an author as saying, "Using genetic engineering to enhance our bodies seems wrong," when he or she intended to say, "Using genetic engineering to enhance our bodies seems wrong, only until you stop and realize that we have already been using technology to enhance our eyes, ears, limbs, and teeth for decades." This is called taking information out of context. This is using supporting evidence unfairly.

3. *Give credit where credit is due.* Giving credit is known as citing. You must use citations when you use someone else's information, but not every piece of supporting information needs a citation.

   - If the supporting information is general knowledge—that is, it can be found in many sources—you do not have to cite your source.
   - If you directly quote a source, you must cite it.
   - If you paraphrase information from a specific source, you must cite it.

If you do not use citations where you should, you are *plagiarizing*—or stealing—someone else's work.

Citing Your Sources

There are a number of ways to cite your sources. Your teacher will probably want you to do it in one of three ways:

- Informal: As in the example in number 1 above, tell where you got the information as you present it in the text of your essay.
- Informal list: At the end of your essay, place an unnumbered list of all the sources you used. This tells the reader where, in general, your information came from.
- Formal: Use numbered footnotes. Footnotes are generally placed at the end of an article or essay, although they may be placed elsewhere depending on your teacher's requirements.

Works Cited

Wambugu, Florence. Testimony before the U.S. House Committee on Agriculture, Washington D.C. 26 Mar. 2003

Using MLA Style to Create a Works Cited List

You will probably need to create a list of works cited for your paper. These include materials that you quoted from, relied heavily on, or consulted to write your paper. There are several different ways to structure these references. The following examples are based on Modern Language Association (MLA) style, one of the major citation styles used by writers.

Book Entries

For most book entries you will need the author's name, the book's title, where it was published, what company published it, and the year it was published. This information is usually found on the inside of the book. Variations on book entries include the following:

A Book by a Single Author
Guest, Emma. *Children of AIDS: Africa's Orphan Crisis.* London: Sterling, 2003.

Two or More Books by the Same Author
Friedman, Thomas L. *The World Is Flat: A Brief History of the Twentieth Century.* New York: Farrar, Straus and Giroux, 2005.

---. *From Beirut to Jerusalem.* New York: Doubleday, 1989.

A Book by Two or More Authors
Pojman, Louis P., and Jeffrey Reiman. *The Death Penalty: For and Against.* Lanham, MD: Rowman & Littlefield, 1998.

A Book with an Editor

> Friedman, Lauri S., ed. *At Issue: What Motivates Suicide Bombers?* San Diego, CA: Greenhaven, 2004.

Periodical and Newspaper Entries

Entries for sources found in periodicals and newspapers are cited a bit differently than books. For one, these sources usually have a title and a publication name. They also may have specific dates and page numbers. Unlike book entries, you do not need to list where newspapers or periodicals are published or what company publishes them.

An Article from a Periodical

> Snow, Keith Harmon. "State Terror in Ethiopia." *Z Magazine* June 2004: 33–35.

An Unsigned Article from a Periodical

> "Broadcast Decency Rules." *Issues & Controversies on File* 30 Apr. 2004.

An Article from a Newspaper

> Constantino, Rebecca. "Fostering Love, Respecting Race." *Los Angeles Times* 14 Dec. 2002: B17.

Internet Sources

To document a source you found online, try to provide as much information on it as possible, including the author's name, the title of the document, date of publication or of last revision, the URL, and your date of access.

A Web Source

> Shyovitz, David. "The History and Development of Yiddish." Jewish Virtual Library. 30 May 2005 < http://www.jewishvirtuallibrary.org/jsource/History/yiddish.html. >. Accessed September 11, 2007.

Your teacher will tell you exactly how information should be cited in your essay. Generally, the very least information needed is the original author's name and the name of the article or other publication.

Be sure you know exactly what information your teacher requires before you start looking for your supporting information so that you know what information to include with your notes.

Sample Essay Topics

Persuasive Essay Topics

Genetic Engineering Is Ethical

Genetic Engineering Is Unethical

Genetic Engineering Can Improve Human Lives

Genetic Engineering Should Not Be Used to Improve Human Lives

Stem Cell Lines Should Be Made Available for Research

Stem Cell Lines Should Not Be Made Available for Research

Genetic Engineering Disadvantages the Poor

Genetic Engineering Will Soon Become Commonplace

Genetic Engineering Can Prevent Disease

Genetic Engineering Violates the Natural Order

Genetically Modified Foods Are Beneficial for Human Health

Genetically Modified Foods Are Dangerous to Human Health

Genetically Modified Foods Can Help Developing Nations

Genetically Modified Foods Keep Developing Nations Hungry

Genetically Modified Foods Threaten the Environment

Genetically Modified Foods Do Not Threaten the Environment

It Is Immoral to Genetically Engineer Animals

Genetically Engineering Animals Can Have Great Medical Benefits for Humans

Parents Should Be Able to Design Their Children's Characteristics

Parents Should Not Be Able to Design Their Children's Characteristics

Parents Should Be Able to Choose the Sex of Their Child

Allowing Parents to Choose the Sex of Their Child Is Dangerous for the Human Race

All Embryos Should Be Screened for Genetically Inherited Disease

All Children Should Be Loved Equally Regardless of Whether They Inherit Disease

Expository Essay Topics

The ABC's of Genetic Engineering

Understanding Differences between Somatic Gene Therapy and Germ Line Engineering

How Do Researchers Use Genetic Engineering to Screen Out Inherited Disease?

Examining What Genetic Engineers Can Do

Examining the Future of Genetic Engineering

Organizations to Contact

Alliance for Bio-Integrity
2040 Pearl Lane, Suite 2, Fairfield, IA 52556 • (206) 888-4852 • e-mail: info@biointegrity.org • Web site: www.biointegrity.org

The Alliance for Bio-Integrity is a nonprofit organization that opposes the use of genetic engineering in agriculture and works to educate the public about the dangers of genetically modified foods. Position papers that argue against genetic engineering from legal, religious, and scientific perspectives—including "Why Concerns about Health Risks of Genetically Engineered Food Are Scientifically Justified"—are available on its Web site.

American Anti-Vivisection Society
801 Old York Rd., Suite 204, Jenkintown, PA 19046-1685 • (215) 887-0816 • fax: (215) 887-2088 • e-mail: aavsonline@aol.com • Web site: http://www.aavs.org

The oldest animal rights group in America, the society opposes all animal experimentation. It publishes educational pamphlets and the quarterly AV magazine.

American Medical Association (AMA)
515 N. State St., Chicago, IL 60610 • (800) 621-8335 • Web site: http://www.ama-assn.org

The AMA is the largest professional association for medical doctors. It helps set standards for medical education and practices, and it is a powerful lobby in Washington for physicians' interests. The association publishes journals for many medical fields, including the monthly Archives of Surgery and the weekly JAMA.

American Society of Law, Medicine, and Ethics (ASLME)

765 Commonwealth Ave., 16th Fl., Boston, MA 02215 • (617) 262-4990 • fax: (617) 437-7596 • e-mail: aslme@bu.edu • Web site: http://www.aslme.org

The society's members include physicians, attorneys, health care administrators, and others interested in the relationship between law, medicine, and ethics. It takes no positions but acts as a forum for discussion of issues such as genetic engineering. The organization has an information clearinghouse and a library. It publishes the quarterlies American Journal of Law & Medicine and the Journal of Law, Medicine & Ethics; the periodic ASLME Briefings; and various books.

Biotechnology Industry Organization (BIO)

1225 Eye Street NW, Suite 400, Washington, DC 20005 • (202) 962-9200 • fax: (202) 962-9201 • e-mail: info@bio.org • Web site: www.bio.org

BIO represents biotechnology companies, academic institutions, state biotechnology centers, and related organizations that support the use of biotechnology in improving health care, agriculture, efforts to clean up the environment, and other fields. BIO publishes fact sheets, backgrounders, and position papers on various issues related to genetic engineering, Including "Facts and Fiction About Plant and Animal Biotechnology."

Center for Bioethics and Human Dignity (CBHD)

2065 Half Day Rd., Bannockburn, IL 60015 • (847) 317-8180 • fax: (847) 317-8101 • e-mail: info@cbhd.org • Web site: www.cbhd.org

CBHD is an international education center whose purpose is to bring Christian perspectives to bear on contemporary bioethical challenges facing society. Its publications address genetic technologies as well as other topics such as euthanasia and abortion. The articles "Biotechnology's Brave New World" and "To Clone or Not to Clone?" are available on its Web site.

Center for Genetics and Society

436 Fourteenth Street, Suite 1302, Oakland, CA 94612 • (510) 625-0819 • fax: 1-510-625-0874 • Web site: www.genetics-and-society.org

The center is a nonprofit organization that advocates for the responsible use of genetic technology in the areas of health care, human reproduction, and agriculture. It favors a cautious approach, including bans on the use of some genetic technologies that it deems threatening to public safety and human rights. Its Web site contains informational and opinionated articles on human genetic engineering as well as the results of numerous public opinion polls on the topic.

Council for Biotechnology Information

1225 Eye Street NW, Suite 400, Washington, D.C. 20043-0380 • Phone: (202) 467-6565 • Web site: http://whybiotech.com

The council is an organization made up of biotechnology companies and trade associations. Its purpose is to promote what its members believe are the benefits of biotechnology in agriculture, industry, science, and health care. Its Web site offers numerous reports and FAQs on various topics, including the environmental and economic effects of genetically engineered crops.

Council for Responsible Genetics (CRG)

5 Upland Road, Suite 3, Cambridge, MA 02140 • (617) 868-0870 • fax: (617) 491-5344 • e-mail: crg@gene-watch.org • Web site: www.gene-watch.org

CRG is a national nonprofit organization of scientists, public health advocates, and others who promote a comprehensive public interest agenda for biotechnology. Its members work to raise public awareness about genetic discrimination, patenting life forms, food safety, and environmental quality. CRG publishes *GeneWatch* magazine, providing access to current and archived articles on its Web site.

Foundation for Biomedical Research

818 Connecticut Ave. NW, Suite 900, Washington, DC 20006 • (202) 457-0654 • fax: (202) 457-0659 • e-mail: info@fbresearch.org • Web site: http://www.fbresearch.org

The foundation supports humane animal research and serves to inform and educate the public about the necessity and importance of laboratory animals in biomedical research and testing. It publishes a bimonthly newsletter, videos, films, and numerous background papers, including "The Use of Animals in Biomedical Research" and "Testing and Caring for Laboratory Animals."

Foundation on Economic Trends (FET)

1660 L St. NW, Suite 216, Washington, DC 20036 • (202) 466-2823 • fax (202) 429-9602 • e-mail: office@ foet.org • Web site: www.foet.org

Founded by science critic and author Jeremy Rifkin, the foundation is a nonprofit organization whose mission is to examine emerging trends in science and technology and their impacts on the environment, the economy, culture, and society. FET works to educate the public about topics such as gene patenting, commercial eugenics, genetic discrimination, and genetically altered food. Its Web site contains news updates and articles, including "Shopping for Humans" and "Unknown Risks of Genetically Engineered Crops."

Friends of the Earth (FOE)

1717 Massachusetts Avenue NW, Suite 600, Washington, DC 20036-2002 • (877) 843-8687 • fax: (202) 783-0444 • e-mail: foe@foe.org • Web site: www.foe.org

Founded in San Francisco in 1969 by David Brower, Friends of the Earth is a grassroots organization whose goal is to create a healthier, more just world. FOE members founded the world's largest federation of democratically elected environmental groups, Friends of the Earth International. Among other efforts, FOE conducted lab tests confirming that genetically engineered corn not approved for human consumption was in products on supermarket shelves across the nation. FOE publishes the quarterly newsmagazine *Friends of the Earth*, current and archived issues of which are available on its Web site.

The Hastings Center

21 Malcolm Gordon Road, Garrison, NY 10524-5555 • (845) 424-4040 • fax: (845) 424-4545 • e-mail: mail@thehastingscenter.org • Web site: www. thehastingscenter.org

The Hastings Center is an independent research institute that explores the medical, ethical, and social ramifications of biomedical advances. The center publishes books, including *Reprogenetics*, the bimonthly *Hastings Center Report*, and the bimonthly newsletter *IRB: Ethics & Human Research*.

National Institutes of Health

National Human Genome Research Institute (NHGRI) 9000 Rockville Pike, Bethesda, MD 20892 • (301) 402-0911 • fax: (301) 402-2218 • Web site: www.nhgri.nih. gov

NIH is the federal government's primary agency for the support of biomedical research. As a division of NIH, NHGRI's mission was to head the Human Genome Project, the federally funded effort to map all human genes, which was completed in April 2003. Now, NHGRI has moved into the genomic era with research aimed at improving human health and fighting disease. Information on the Project and relevant articles are available on its Web site.

Organic Consumers Association (OCA)

6101 Cliff Estate Road, Little Marais, MN 55614 • (218) 226-4164 • fax: (218) 353-7652 • Web site: www. organicconsumers.org

The OCA promotes food safety, organic farming, and sustainable agriculture practices. It provides information on the hazards of genetically engineered food, irradiated food, food grown with toxic sludge fertilizer, mad cow disease, rBGH in milk, and other issues, and organizes boycotts and protests around these issues. It publishes *BioDemocracy News* and its Web site includes many fact sheets and articles on genetically modified foods.

People for the Ethical Treatment of Animals (PETA)

501 Front St., Norfolk, VA 23510 • (757) 622-PETA (7382) • fax: (757) 622-0457 • Web site: http://www. peta-online.org

PETA is an educational, activist group that opposes all forms of animal exploitation, including genetic engineering experiments on animals. It conducts rallies and demonstrations to focus attention on animal experimentation. It publishes reports on animal experimentation and animal farming and the periodic People for the Ethical Treatment of Animals—Action Alerts.

President's Council on Bioethics

1801 Pennsylvania Avenue NW, Suite 700, Washington, DC 20006 • (202) 296-4669 • e-mail: info@bioethics.gov • Web site: www.bioethics.gov

When the National Bioethics Advisory Commission's charter expired in October 2001, President George Bush established the President's Council on Bioethics. It works to protect the rights and welfare of human research subjects and govern the management and use of genetic information. On its Web site, the Council provides access to its report "Beyond Therapy: Biotechnology and the Pursuit of Happiness."

U.S. Department of Agriculture (USDA)

1400 Independence Ave. SW, Washington, DC 20250 • Web site on agricultural biotechnology: www.nal.usda.gov/bic

The USDA is one of three federal agencies, along with the Environmental Protection Agency (EPA) and the U.S. Food and Drug Administration (FDA), primarily responsible for regulating biotechnology in the United States. The USDA conducts research on the safety of genetically engineered organisms, helps form government policy on agricultural biotechnology, and provides information to the public about these technologies.

Bibliography

Books

John C. Avise, *The Hope, Hype, and Reality of Genetic Engineering: Remarkable Stories from Agriculture, Industry, Medicine, and the Environment*. New York: Oxford University Press, 2004.

Andrew Kimbrell, Your Right to Know: Genetic Engineering and the Secret Changes in Your Food. San Rafael, CA: Earth Aware Editions, 2007.

Bill McKibben, *Enough: Staying Human in an Engineered Age*. New York: Henry Holt, 2003.

Maxwell J. Mehlman, *Wondergenes: Genetic Enhancement and the Future of Society.* Bloomington: Indiana University Press, 2003.

Stephen Nottingham, *Eat Your Genes: How Genetically Modified Food is Entering Our Diet*. London: Zed, 2003.

Ted Peters, *Playing God? Genetic Determinism and Human Freedom*. New York: Routledge, 2003.

Pamela C. Ronald and R. W. Adamchak, *Tomorrow's Table: A Marriage of Genetic Engineering and Organic Farming.* New York: Oxford University Press, 2007.

Michael J. Sandel, *The Case against Perfection: Ethics in the Age of Genetic Engineering*. Belknap Press, 2007.

Lee M. Silver, *Remaking Eden: How Genetic Engineering and Cloning Will Transform the American Family.* New York: Harper Perennial, 2007.

Jennifer A. Thomson, *Seeds for the Future: The Impact of Genetically Modified Crops on the Environment.* New York: Cornell University Press, 2007.

Periodicals

Rosie Aiello, "Cloning could save endangered species," *McGill Daily*, Volume 95, Number 27, January 9, 2006. http://www.mcgilldaily.com/view.php?aid = 4673

Michael de Alessi, "Saving Endangered Species Privately: A Case Study of Earth Sanctuaries, LTD," Pacific Research Institute, August 2003. http://www.perc.org/pdf/earth_sanct.pdf

Francoise Baylis and Jason Scott Robert, "The Inevitability of Genetic Enhancement Technologies," *Bioethics*, Vol. 18, No. 1, 2004.

Russell Blackford, "Debunking the Brave New World," www.betterhumans.com, March 24, 2004.

"Conservation Profiles: Landowners Help Imperiled Wildlife," U.S. Fish and Wildlife Service, http://www.fws.gov/endangered/pubs/Safe%20Harbor/SafeHarbor.pdf

"Designer Babies: What Would You Do For A 'Healthy' Baby?" *Science Daily*, September 6, 2006. http://www.sciencedaily.com/releases/2006/09/060905084657.htm

George Dvorsky, "Redesigning Human Bioethics," www.betterhumans.com, January 19, 2003.

Ronald Bailey, "Hooray for Designer Babies!" *Reason*, March 6, 2002. www.reason.com/news/printer/34776.html.

Marcy Darnovsky, "Embryo Cloning and Beyond," *Tikkun*, vol. 17, July/August 2002.

Mark Dodd, "Cows weren't better back then," *NZ Dairy Exporter*, December 2006, p. 76.

Lindsay Fitzclarence, "Sports Frankenstein: character, commerce and cloning," *Arena Magazine*, August-September 2005, p. 14–16.

Mark S. Frankel, "Inheritable Genetic Modification and a Brave New World," *Hastings Center Report,* vol. 33, March/April, 2003.

Greenpeace. "Say No to Genetic Engineering," May 17, 2007. http://www.greenpeace.org/international/campaigns/genetic-engineering

"Has Genetic Engineering Gone Too Far?" *Current Events,* April 16, 2007, p. 7–10.

Karen Hirsch, "Brave New Animals," *Animal Issues,* Spring 2003.

David Kennell, "Genetically Engineered Plant Crops: Potential for Disaster," *Synthesis/Regeneration,* Fall 2004, p. 11.

Chuck Klosterman, "The Awe-Inspiring Majesty of Science: If Tampering with the DNA of Unborn Children in an Attempt to Grant Them Unfathomable Superpowers Is Wrong, I Don't Wanna Be Right." *Esquire,* October 2004, p. 108–110.

Erika Jonietz, "Choosing Our Children's Genetic Futures," *Technology Review,* February 2003.

Tim Lewthwaite, "Time Is Running Out: Reproductive Technology and the Race to Save Endangered Species," *Communique,* March 2005. http://www.aza.org/Publications/2005/03/TimeRunningOutSidebar.pdf

Carol Milano, "What's Happening to Your Food? How Genetic Engineering Is Changing What's on Your Plate," *Current Health 2,* April-May 2007, p 8–12.

Anuradha Mittal, "Biotechnology and the Third World: A Question of Social Morality," June 5, 2003, www.foodfirst.org.

Isaac M. Mwase, "Genetic Enhancement and the Fate of the Worse Off," *Kennedy Institute of Ethics Journal* Johns Hopkins University Press Vol. 15, No. 1, 2005, p. 83–89.

Channapatna S. Prakash and Gregory Conko, "Looking at GM Crops from a Historical Perspective," *Celebrating 50 Years of DNA: 1953–2003*, London Business Weekly, 2003.

Gyorgy Scrinis, "Engineering the Foodchain," *Arena Magazine*, June-July 2005, p 37–40.

The Sierra Club. "Banned Abroad, Sold in the U.S.!!! Genetically Engineered Food." July 1, 2001, www.sierraclub.org.

Jeffrey M. Smith, "Genetically Engineered Crops May Cause Human Disease," *Rachel's Democracy & Health News*, Iss. 870, August 31, 2006.

Lisa Turner, "Playing with Our Food," *Better Nutrition*, April 2007, p. 30.

Alison L. Van Eenennaam, "Genetic Engineering and Animal Agriculture," University of California, Division of Agriculture and National Resources, Publication No. 8184, Genetic Engineering Fact Sheet 7, 2005. http://anrcatalog/ucdavis.edu/pdf/8184.pdf

Matthew Wells, "Louisiana's Frozen Ark," BBC News, May 18, 2005. http://news.bbc.co.uk/1/hi/sci/tech/4547533.stm

Florence Wambugu, Testimony before the U.S. House Committee on Agriculture, Washington D.C., March 26, 2003.

Arlene Weintraub, "Crossing the Gene Barrier; On the Frontiers of Biotech, Two Scientists Are Mingling the Genetic Materials of Man and Beast in New Ways. The Hoped-For Outcome: Radical Treatments for Some of Mankind's Most Intractable Ailments," *Business Week*, January 16, 2006, p 72.

Websites

BetterHumans.com (www.betterhumans.com). A collection of works that advocate the use of science and technology for improving human beings. It supports the genetic engineering of humans, plants, animals, and contains articles on a wide variety of angles relating to these topics.

Genetic Engineering Organization (www.geneticengineering.org). Geenor attempts to increase public awareness about genetic engineering through online articles and software.

Genetic Engineering Network (www.geneticsaction.org.uk). This organization's website, based in the United Kingdom, contains a plethora of information on why genetic engineering efforts on humans, plants and animals should be opposed.

Genetic Engineering News (www.genengnews.com). A web site devoted exclusively to breaking stories relating to genetic engineering.

Greenpeace (www.greenpeace.org). Genetic engineering is just one of the many issues the environmental organization Greenpeace concentrates its efforts on. Greenpeace opposes genetically modified crops and seeds on the grounds that it perpetuates world hunger and exploits local communities.

Index

Picture Credits

About the Editor

Lauri S. Friedman earned her bachelor's degree in religion and political science from Vassar College in Poughkeepsie, NY. Her studies there focused on political Islam. Friedman has worked as a non-fiction writer, a newspaper journalist, and an editor for more than 7 years. She has accumulated extensive experience in both academic and professional settings.

Friedman has edited and authored numerous publications for Greenhaven Press on controversial social issues such as gay marriage, Islam, energy, discrimination, suicide bombers, and the war on terror. Much of the *Writing the Critical Essay* series has been under her direction or authorship. She was instrumental in the creation of the series, and played a critical role in its conception and development.